Dearest Shelley:

We love you & feel that in your loving way, you are our own "Remarkable Latter-day Saint Woman".

God bless you always—

Dad & Mamma.

xxx

April 1980

Remarkable
Stories
from the
Latter-day Saints

Volume 1

Remarkable Stories from the Lives of Latter-day Saint Women

Volume II

Compiled by Leon R. Hartshorn

Published by Deseret Book Company, Salt Lake City, Utah, 1978

Library of Congress Catalog Card No. 75-23943
ISBN 0-87747-569-5

Lithographed by

DESERET PRESS

in the United States of America

Contents

AFTON AFFLECK*

"Faith Is a Gift of God"

On December 19, 1949, I was preparing for a wonderful Christmas party, to which Bob and I had invited many of our friends and neighbors. I wanted it to be so lovely, but as I was working on some of the preparations, I had a headache that kept getting more severe. I tried several times in the afternoon to reach Bob. A voice said to me, "You have spinal meningitis," and I cried aloud, "Oh, no!" My father had died of spinal meningitis! (Later I learned I not only had spinal meningitis, but encephalitis as well.)

When the doctor came, he lifted up one of my legs and it was as if red and blue lightning had come out of the back of my neck. He said to Bob, "Let's administer to her," so they did. Before we left for the hospital, Bob called President Robert Young of the Salt Lake Temple and asked him to meet us there.

I had put away the children's Christmas presents so they couldn't find them, and as we drove to the hospital I tried to tell Bob where they were. I also tried to tell him where his socks were. We always had a little joke about his socks—I had been

---

*Afton Affleck has served on the YWMIA general board and is now a member of the Youth Correlation Committee of the Church. She was born in Holbrook, Idaho, a daughter of Horace James and Leila Afton Moss Grant. She was married to Robert Charles Affleck on September 5, 1934, in the Salt Lake Temple, and they have had five children, three of whom are living.

putting them in the same drawer all our married life, but he could never find them. I remember regaining consciousness on the way to the hospital and finally being able to tell him where they were.

At the hospital President Young and Bob administered to me and I heard them, though I was unconscious. President Young rebuked the disease to have no power to distort my body, and promised me that I would be made whole. He blessed me that I would have the strength to undergo the suffering that would be mine to bear.

During the time in isolation, where I suffered severely, I learned a great deal about the Savior, the atonement, and the love of the Lord Jesus Christ. It seemed to me that I was being taught constantly. There was only one time that I felt I could not endure the pain, but at that very moment Uncle Ray Moss and his son Raphel put their hands on my head and administered to me.

During this time I had such terrible pain in my eyes that I could not see. Once I regained consciousness long enough to hear a doctor telling his sister, who was his technician, that I had one chance in five thousand of ever seeing—but I knew I would see. In addition, my right side was affected; I could not move my foot, and my arm had become weakened. But I never doubted that I would be made whole.

One night I thought I was standing before a polished granite mountain. A voice said to me, "If you have faith even a thousandth the size of a grain of sand, you can move your foot and you can see." I felt rebuked, because I thought I had already exercised great faith.

Mother was president of the South Davis Stake Relief Society, and before one of the Singing Mothers practices, all the members fasted all day for me. The Parleys Ward M Men and Gleaners fasted for twenty-four hours and then met together to pray for me. Later I learned that after the last session in the Salt Lake Temple one evening, the temple presidency went to a room and knelt in prayer in my behalf.

I prayed to the Lord and I exercised faith. Then I tried to turn my head. Up to then I had not been able to do so without losing consciousness, but this time I was able to turn it and could see a sliver of light under my door.

I also felt that if I tried, I could move my leg. My mind

went back to the day before I became sick. I was at the temple, and a Sister Ogden, a temple worker, had come to me and said, "Sister Affleck, I feel I should tell you a story." She continued, "I was on crutches for years. My husband and I went to Hawaii, and while there we went to the temple. The officiators made a place for me at the front and said, when it was time for the prayer circle, 'Sister Ogden, come to the prayer circle.' I answered, 'I cannot walk, and someone has taken my crutches.' 'We took your crutches,' said one of the officiators. 'Did you not come here to be healed?' "

Just then, she said, she felt a great crunching in her ankle—almost more than she could stand. Then she had faith to stand erect and walk up to the front of the room. Sister Ogden did not know how soon I would use that story to bring forth all of the faith within me.

Faith is a gift of God, and he granted me more faith than I had ever had in my life. I *did* move my leg. I lay there the rest of the night rejoicing and praising the Lord—I did not want to tell anyone until morning. The Lord had promised that I would be healed through faith and the power of the priesthood and the prayers of those who loved me. I praise the Lord for allowing me to have that kind of experience, because it strengthened me.

Oral History Program, Church Historical Department, Salt Lake City, Utah, 1972, pp. 26-28.

CORA HILL ARNOLD*

"Her Face Lighted Up"

I didn't like her! I don't know why. I just simply didn't like her. I am sure those who study these things would have said it was a personality clash. I found fault with everything she did—not always to myself, I am ashamed to admit. I heard from others that she felt the same way about me. She seemed always to force herself into the limelight, to show everyone how important she was. How I disliked to see her achieve!

She was never very friendly to me, and I would pass her with a cold nod or a polite hello. When I thought about her— which was too often—I was miserable because to dislike a person does make one unhappy.

And then one day I heard she was ill. So what? It was not my worry.

But it was, and I couldn't forget it because I have an active conscience. I finally went into my kitchen and stirred up some applesauce cupcakes and swirled on a favorite frosting, not forgetting colored candies for the top.

*Cora Hill Arnold was born in Wellington, Carbon County, Utah, and was graduated from Carbon High School and LDS Business College. She was married to Albert Henry Arnold in the Salt Lake Temple, and they have two sons, Roger and Thomas, and four grandchildren. Currently treasurer of the Utah State Poetry Society, Sister Arnold lives in Salt Lake City.

4

And I took them to her!

Her face lighted up with surprise and pleasure, and a warm glow spread over my heart, washing away the angry prejudice at once. As I walked from her home to mine I was smiling and the day was bright and beautiful.

Now she is one of my close friends. We have great fun times together. We have much in common and I have found her to be a most choice person with a delightful sense of humor. She has many talents and is extremely modest about them. When she achieves I glow with pride.

Someone has said, "Hate is love gone wrong. We hate those whom we might have loved."

I only know my loss would have been great had I continued to deem her my enemy.

Relief Society Magazine, January 1968, p. 595.

Biographical Sketch

MARGARET McNEIL BALLARD

Margaret McNeil Ballard was born April 14, 1846, in Tranent, Scotland. Her parents, Thomas and Janet Reid McNeil, joined the Church when Margaret was a little girl and immigrated to Utah in 1856. Margaret married Henry Ballard on May 5, 1861, and they were parents of eleven children. While her husband served as bishop of their ward, she was ward Relief Society president for thirty years. She died on July 21, 1918, at the age of seventy-two.

Of her, we read: "Margaret McNeil Ballard represented the highest type of pioneer womanhood—tough in the face of difficulty, yet tender to all living creatures. However hard the trial, her courage was undaunted, her zeal undampened, her faith unruffled. Hardship, hunger and toil were too long and too frequently her lot, and she endured them without murmuring. Always close to God, she was unusually susceptible to the 'whisperings of the Spirit,' by which she sought to guide her life." (*Melvin J. Ballard, Crusader for Righteousness* [Bookcraft, 1968], p. 23.)

MARGARET McNEIL
BALLARD

"My Brother James"

My father was advised to go to St. Louis to spend the winter there and prepare to go on to Utah the next year. But instead of staying in St. Louis, he was called on a mission to help a settlement one hundred miles west of civilization. The place was to be called Genoa. We left St. Louis on the steamboat and came up the Mississippi River. The measles broke out while we were on the boat and all of my brothers and sisters got them and were very sick, with the exception of myself. When we landed we camped on the bank of the river until our teams and wagons came.

When we were ready to start on our journey westward, my father's team, consisting of unbroken, five-year-old oxen, ran away, so our family was delayed. My father had never seen oxen before and the animals allotted to him had to be roped and tied to get the yoke on them and fastened to the wagon. As soon as they had been released from the ropes, they had become unmanageable and run away.

The main company had gone on ahead and my mother was anxious to have me go with them, so she strapped my little brother James on my back with a shawl and sent us along. James was only four years old and was still quite sick with the measles, but Mother had all she could do to care for the other children. We traveled all day, and that night a kind lady helped me take my brother off my back. I sat up alone, all night, and held James on my lap with a shawl wrapped around him. He was a little better in the morning. The people in the camp were very good to us and gave us a little fried bacon and some bread for breakfast.

We traveled this way for about a week, my brother and I not seeing our mother during this time. Each morning one of the men would write a note and put it in the slit of a willow stuck into the ground, to tell the party coming behind how we were getting along. In this way mother knew that we were alright.

Autobiography of Margaret McNeil Ballard, pp. 2-3. (Unpublished manuscript.)

"I Walked Every Step of the Way"

While crossing the plains my mother's health was very poor, so I tried to assist her as much as I could. Every morning I would get up early and get breakfast for the family and milk my cow so that I could hurry and drive her on ahead of the company. I would let her eat in all grassy places until the company had passed on ahead and then I would hurry and catch up with them. The cow furnished us with milk, our chief source of food, and it was very important to see that she was fed as well as circumstances would permit. Had it not been for this we would have starved.

Being alone much of the time, I had to get across the rivers the best I could. Our cow was a jersey and had a long tail. When it was necessary to cross a river, I would wind the end of the cow's tail around my hand and swim across with her. At the end of each day's journey I would milk her and help prepare our supper and then would be glad to go to sleep wherever my bed happened to be. . . .

Our food gave out and we had nothing but milk and wild rose berries to eat. However, we had a good team and could travel fast. We arrived in Ogden on the fourth day of October, after a journey of hardships and hunger, with thankfulness to our Heavenly Father for his protecting care. I walked every step of the way across the plains and drove my cow, and a large part of the way I carried my little brother James on my back.

We camped on the outskirts of town and Father left us and went into Ogden to find work. While camping here many people passed us on their way to attend the general conference of the Church, held in Salt Lake City.

Across the field from where we camped was a little house, and out in the yard was a big pile of squash. We were all nearly starved to death and my mother sent me over to this place to beg a squash, for we did not have a cent of money. Some of the children were very weak for the want of food. I knocked at the door and an old lady came and said, "Come in, come in. I knew you were coming and have been told to give you food." She gave me a large loaf of fresh bread and said to tell my mother that she would come over soon. It was not long until she came and brought us a nice cooked dinner, something we had not had for a long time. The woman was surely inspired of the Lord to help us, and we were indeed grateful for her kindness.

When Father came back to us, he had found a man whom he had known in Scotland. This man took us to his home and we stayed there until we were ready to go to Cache Valley. We all were put to work. Mother took the smaller children and went and husked corn. I herded cattle, and Father and my older brothers worked on the threshing machines.

When we had a sufficient supply, we left Ogden and had not gone far before we met Henry Ballard and Aaron Dewitt, who had been to conference and were returning to their homes in Cache Valley. This was my first meeting with the man who would be my husband. At the time of this meeting I was a bare-foot, sunburned little girl driving my cow along the dusty county road, but it was made known to my mother and to Henry at that time that I would someday be his wife.

Autobiography of Margaret McNeil Ballard, pp. 4-6.

———◆———

MARGARET McNEIL BALLARD

"Courting in Pioneer Days"

In January Brother Ballard asked me to go to a dance with him over to Providence, a little village several miles from Logan. We had a yoke of oxen and a heavy sleigh and it was very cold. It snowed about three feet while we were at the dance. We could not come home, so we sat up all the rest of the night, for there was not room for very many of us to go to bed in the little log house. We had a very hard time getting home the next day. So you see, courting even in pioneer days had its hardships.

I had been keeping company with Brother Ballard for some time, and although I was but fifteen years old, he wanted me to marry him. He felt that he could take care of and provide for me without my having to work as hard as I had been working. We were married on May 5, 1861. He was sustained as bishop of the Logan Second Ward on April 14 of that year, a position he held for nearly forty years. During that time I always endeavored to assist him and encourage him in his work.

Autobiography of Margaret McNeil Ballard, p. 7.

◄――――►

MARGARET McNEIL BALLARD

"Two Little Dresses"

A short time before my first baby was born, I had my first experience in sewing. My husband had a fine young steer that he was saving to sell in order to get enough money for us to buy material to make clothes for the new little baby that we were expecting. One of the prominent brethren of Logan suffered a great financial loss at this time and was left destitute. The people were called upon to give what they could for the support of the unfortunate family. We had our winter's supply of food in the house, but no money, so the steer was the only thing we could dispose of to raise money.

My husband came home feeling bad and said, "Margaret, I am very sorry and disappointed, but I have been called upon to raise some money to help out one of our brethren, and the only thing I have that I can give is that steer. What shall I do?" I too was very much disappointed but said, "Give it, Henry. We will find a way." My husband's gratitude for my willingness and his regrets brought him to tears. It was a big sacrifice for me at the time, but I knew it was right.

After my husband had left the house, I hunted out two of his old homespun woolen shirts and pulled down the blinds and locked the doors so that no one would see me try my hand at a new art. I spread the shirts on the floor and, without a pattern, cut out the two little dresses and sewed them up by hand. This was about all the clothing I had for my first child. However, she was most welcome to us and was given as much love as two loving parents were capable of bestowing.

Our first baby was born on January 18, 1863. It was a girl and we named her Margaret Hannah. At the time of her birth my husband was the proudest father in the valley.

Autobiography of Margaret McNeil Ballard, pp. 8-9.

MARGARET McNEIL BALLARD

"Blessed Abundantly"

On May 17, 1884, the Logan Temple was dedicated. The second day after the dedication President John Taylor said that all members of the Church who were worthy and who desired to go through the temple might do so the next day.

My husband, being bishop, was very busy writing out recommends for all who wished to go through the temple, when my daughter came in with a newspaper in her hand and asked

13

for her father. I told her that he was very busy, but to give the paper to me and I would give it to him. She said, "No, a man gave the paper to me and told me to give it to no one but Father."

I let the child take the paper to her father, and when he took it and looked at it he was greatly surprised, for he saw that the paper had been printed in Berkshire, England, his birthplace, and was only four days old. He was so amazed at such an incident that he called Ellen and asked her where the man was who had given her the paper. She said she was playing on the sidewalk with other children when two men came walking down the middle of the street. One of them called to her, saying, "Come here, little girl." She hesitated at first, for there were other little girls with her. Then he pointed to her and said, "You." She went and he gave her the paper and told her to give it to her father.

The paper contained about sixty names of dead acquaintances of my husband, giving the dates of birth and death. My husband took the paper to the president of the temple and asked him what he thought about it. President Merrill said, "Brother Ballard, that was one of the three Nephites or some other person who brought that paper to you, for it could come in no other way in so short a time. It is for you to do the work for them."

My husband was baptized for the men and I for the women, and all of the work was done for them. Again I felt the Lord was mindful of us and blessed us abundantly.

Autobiography of Margaret McNeil Ballard, pp. 11-12.

"You Will Bear a Son"

Melvin Joseph Ballard was a child of promise. He was carried beneath his mother's heart during a period of poverty, of depression, of crop failure, and of sorrow. Melvin's mother had given birth to six children. Two were taken in death while in the first year of their lives, just ten days apart. They were twins, a boy and a girl. Sorrow and sickness had weakened the mother's physical strength, and in the years to follow she lost several children who were born prematurely. Her heart was sore; her arms were empty; and, again, the life of her unborn child was threatened. Many days and weeks she was bedfast; but like Rachel of old, her heart yearned for a child, and she cried to the Lord, "Give me children, else I die."

One day, after her husband had taken the children a block away to see a parade, she raised her trembling body from the bed, crawled to the door, and locked it so that she might pour out her soul to God on her knees in prayer. She called to remembrance her willingness to bear children and her approval of her husband's marriage to her sister, that a greater posterity might build up God's kingdom in Zion. She begged the Lord for help. She felt that she had done all that was in her power, and she asked to know her standing in his sight.

God heard her prayer, and comfort was given to her. She saw no person, but a voice spoke plainly to her, saying, "Be of good cheer. Your life is acceptable, and you will bear a son who will become an apostle of the Lord Jesus Christ."

In due time her child was born. She did bear a son, her last son, and he was named Melvin Joseph. His life was precious in the sight of his father and mother, and they recognized in him a choice spirit. He was also honored by his brothers and sisters, although they did not know of the promise given him.

Bryant S. Hinckley, *Sermons and Missionary Service of Melvin Joseph Ballard* (Deseret Book Co., 1949), pp. 22-23.

"It Comforts Me to Have Done Some Good"

From the first organization of the Relief Society in Cache Valley, until 1880, I labored as a teacher. On December 11, 1880, I was put in as president of this organization in the Second Ward, with Sister Barbara Larsen as first counselor and Sister Susan J. Smith as second counselor, and Sister Emmeline James as secretary. I labored in this capacity for over thirty years. During these years I tried to do my duty in caring for the sick and comforting the needy.

I have walked for blocks through the deep snow; I have been out in rains and winds, in the darkest nights, and in the earliest hours of the morning, to comfort and minister to those who were afflicted and who were sick and suffering and sorrowing and dying. I have sat up all night time after time with the sick, laid out the dead, made burial clothes, mothered the orphans, comforted the widows, and given advice to those in need. I have tried to be a peacemaker to those in trouble and through it all the Lord directed me and I enjoyed His Spirit as my companion in my labors. Many an afflicted one has gone to her last sleep blessing me and many who yet remain bless me for services rendered unto them. It comforts me to have done some good to those less fortunate than myself.

Autobiography of Margaret McNeil Ballard, p. 11.

"I Have Never Ceased My Labors"

My husband died February 26, 1908, after a brief illness. He had suffered for a number of years, and I was thankful to see him released from this suffering. My life has been more lonely without him than anyone can imagine without having experienced it themselves. He was a kind and loving husband, an affectionate father, and a man of honor and justice, filled with faith in God, and he exercised great power in his priesthood. I have been a widow for nine years. Each day I miss him more, and I know that I will be filled with joy when once more I am with him.

I am thankful for my family, for their love and respect, and for the honor they have always shown to me and their father. I am thankful for their obedience and for their desire to follow their parents' example concerning the things of the Lord. I am thankful that the Lord has blessed them with the privilege of every one having been married in the temple by the priesthood of God and sealed for time and eternity—except Edna, who is not yet married.

My life has been one of varied experiences. I have had a great deal of sickness to pass through, with both my children and grandchildren, but I have always relied upon the Lord, and he has never failed me. I have stood by my husband under all conditions: sickness, trials, poverty, and prosperity. I have labored by his side in the fields. I have done various kinds of work, such as soapmaking, weaving and spinning, and sowing, plowing, and gleaning. From the first day that I entered this valley until this day I have never ceased my labors to upbuild and beautify this city.

Although my life has been one of sacrifice and service, I feel that I have lived it the best I could with the knowledge I have had.

My testimony of the truthfulness of the gospel grows stronger each day and the work grows dearer and sweeter to my soul. I know that God lives and that he lives and answers prayer, that Jesus is the Son of the living God, and that Joseph Smith was his prophet. I thank God for this knowledge and leave this as my testimony to my children and grandchildren and all who may come after me.

Autobiography of Margaret McNeil Ballard, pp. 17-19.

MARY BATHGATE

"She Must Get into the Wagon"

(16 August 1856)—Sister Mary
Bathgate was badly bitten by a large rattlesnake, just above the
ankle, on the back part of her leg. She and Sister Isabella Park
were about half a mile ahead of the camp at the time it happened. They were both old women, over sixty years of age, and
neither of them had ridden one inch since they had left Iowa
campground. Sister Bathgate sent a little girl hurrying back to
have me and Brothers Leonard and Crandall come with all
haste, and bring the oil with us, for she was bitten badly.

As soon as we heard the news, we left all things and, with
the oil, we went posthaste. When we got to her she was quite
sick but said that there was power in the priesthood and she
knew it. So we took a pocketknife, cut the wound larger, and
squeezed out all the bad blood we could. We then anointed her
and laid our hands on her in the name of Jesus; we felt to rebuke
the influence of the poison, and she felt full of faith. We then
told her that she must get into the wagon, so she called witnesses
to prove that she did not get into the wagon until she was compelled to because of the cursed snake. We started on and
traveled two miles, then stopped for refreshment. Sister
Bathgate continued to be quite sick but was full of faith, and
after stopping one and one-half hours we hitched up our teams.

As the word was given for the teams to start, old Sister Isabella Park ran to the wagon to see how her companion was. The driver, not seeing her, halloed at his team, and they being quick to mind, Sister Park could not get out of the way, and the fore wheel struck her and threw her down and passed over both her hips. Brother Leonard grabbed hold of her to pull her out of the way before the hind wheel could catch her. He only got her partway and the hind wheel passed over her ankles.

We all thought that she would be all mashed to pieces, but to the joy of us all, there was not a bone broken, although the wagon had something like two tons' burden on it, a load for four yoke of oxen. We went right to work and applied the same medicine to her that we did to the sister who was bitten by the rattlesnake, and although quite sore for a few days, Sister Park got better, so that she was back walking before we got into the Valley, and Sister Bathgate was right by her side, to cheer her up.

LeRoy R. and Ann W. Hafen, *Handcarts to Zion* (Glendale, California: Arthur H. Clark Company, 1960), pp. 108-12.

SALLY BLACK *

"Look, Mommy, I'm Strong!"

One morning I was preparing to attend an auxiliary presidency meeting to be held at my counselor's home. As was my usual procedure, I got our two children—Michelle, three, and Julie, three months old—ready to attend the meeting with me. Then I asked Michelle to stay in the house and sit on the floor by Julie, who was in her infant seat, while I backed the car out of the garage. I explained that I would be right back to get them. I had done this regularly when the weather was cold.

That morning as I opened the garage door, entered the car, and started it, a strong feeling came over me, telling me not to back the car out of the garage. Since I had done this same thing so many times before, I pushed the thought aside; however, again, I felt the strong feeling that I should not back the car out. Finally realizing that I should heed the prompting, I got out of the car to go back into the house, and found Michelle pushing against the rear bumper of the car, hidden from my view. "Look, Mommy, I'm strong!" she said. "The car can't move!"

*Sally Nielsen Black and her husband, O. Brent Black, are parents of three children, Kenneth, Michelle, and Julie. A graduate of the University of Utah, she has served in YWMIA and Relief Society presidencies and twice as a stake YWMIA president. She is now a member of the Youth Correlation Committee of the Church.

GLENDA BRADY*

"As Though He Could See"

In 1954 we were living in Mexico City, where Dad was a medical student. Since we were in Mexico on a student visa, it seemed that there was perpetual red tape to deal with. I had a younger brother, Mark, who was seven at the time, and a blind brother, Virgil, who was thirteen. They were inseparable pals in Mexico.

One morning Dad gave the two boys instructions to go downtown and wait in line to get some immigration problems taken care of. Since Mother was not feeling well, the boys were to go and wait in line, then she would come down and get the work done once they finally got to the window. (Anyone familiar with Mexico knows the endless hours one can wait in line to see a minor secretary or to be told that one is in the wrong line!)

Dad's further instructions were that when Mom arrived they were to go home immediately and begin their studies and practicing for the day. (Dad taught us our schoolwork at home, and we were also required to practice our musical instruments, three instruments each, one hour on each instrument per day.)

*Glenda Mae Haws Brady, the oldest of eight children, was born in the Mormon colonies in Chihuahua, Mexico. In 1960 she married Robert Nyle Brady, who is presently serving as a stake president in Tennessee. They are the parents of three children and reside in Brentwood, Tennessee.

22

Virgil and Mark had been waiting in the line for about three hours and were still a long way from the window when Mother arrived looking pale and feeling weak. She told them to go home and get their work done, that she would stay and complete the immigration business.

The boys walked through the crowded city streets to the bus stop three blocks away. When their bus pulled up, Mark yelled to Virgil, "Hurry, here it is," and he began jostling with the crowds who also wanted to get on the bus. Virgil hesitated— but when you hesitate in a Mexico City crowd, you are lost. They missed the bus and Mark began to murmur against his older brother. Then, after a few moments, a second bus came. Mark again took Virgil's arm and said, "Get ready now, Virgil, here it is."

They pushed through the crowd and were beginning to get onto the bus when Virgil pulled back. The crowd was bustling to get around them and yelling that they were in the way. Again Mark cried, "Come on, Virgil!" But Virgil just stood without saying a word—something was perplexing him.

When a third bus came, immediately afterward, Mark was sure that they could get on it since there was no crowd to hinder them. The driver pulled over and opened the door. Mark assumed that Virgil was right behind him, but when he turned around, he saw Virgil running through the crowd, dodging people as though he could see. As the bus driver shouted at them angrily, Mark jumped off the bus to pursue Virgil.

When he rounded the corner and entered the immigration office, Mark saw Virgil run up to Mother, find her in the crowd, and put his hand firmly on her shoulder just as she was about to faint. She left Virgil standing in line while she slumped onto a nearby bench. Afraid for having disobeyed, my younger brother ran over to Mother to explain that Virgil just wouldn't get on the buses. She merely replied, "I'm so glad you came back."

It was only later that we all realized that the Spirit had carried the message of her three separate prayers to Virgil. Virgil heard and understood the promptings clearly and acted with the determination that was so characteristic of him.

◄——►

JANET W. BREEZE

"The Little White Box"

One of the early memories of my childhood concerns the subject of tithing. I was four. My father had just passed away, and my mother had taken employment in a downtown department store. I don't remember how the subject came up, but I vividly remember Mother saying, "You have more money when you pay your tithing."

Like a typical four-going-on-five, I asked, "How come?"

"Because," she said, "when you give the Lord his money first, that leaves you with less. With less money, you watch it more closely. And when you avoid spending money foolishly, you have more."

Even though I still didn't know the difference between a dime and a dollar, outside of their physical size, what my mother said made sense. But, like a good teacher who recognizes the value of repetition, she made certain that the first time she told me was not the last time she told me. And, as I grew older, I was encouraged to make my first "little white box."

It turned out to be quite a production. I painted it with fancy flowers; and on the center of the lid, in macaroni alphabets, I glued the letters T-I-T-H-I-N-G.

Even though, as I became a career girl, the little white box was later replaced by numbers in an account book and checkbook, by the time I entered marriage, tithing was a natural and acceptable part of my life. Since then, things have happened that have convinced me more thoroughly than ever that the Lord does bless us when we comply with the things he asks of us.

One of many incidents stands out in my mind. It was shortly after our first baby was born. My husband was an enlisted man in the army. We lived comfortably, but somehow the money we had just didn't seem to want to stretch into the shape of baby furniture, and we were too far away from home to borrow a crib from relatives. Since babies have to have someplace to sleep, it was a temptation to buy a crib rather than pay our tithing. But we didn't give in.

Then a mysterious letter came in the mail. From the Department of the Army, it was addressed to me. It stated that through some oversight, my allotment checks had not started as soon as they should have. Enclosed was a check correcting the error made over a year before. Even though it was money we should have received anyway, we deemed it a great blessing that it had somehow been saved until a time when we could better use it.

This was just one occasion. There have been other times when unexpected blessings have come to us.

I am sure that the Lord does not bless everyone in exactly the same way. However, whether it has been the result of Mother's practical view toward tithing, or unexpected sources of income, we feel very strongly that our blessing for the payment of tithing has been financial security.

Now it is our duty to share this wonderful law of tithing with our children. As soon as that first precious baby grew into a little girl with a piggy bank, we told her about tithing. At that time, we had a weekly family home evening that consisted of a story about Jesus, ring-around-the rosy, and an ice cream cone. One night, before the ice cream cone, we sat at the kitchen table and, with white paper, glue, and crayons, decorated a "little white box," which read "Claudia's Tithing." Thereafter, each family home evening Daddy would give her ten pennies. One penny was to go in the little white box and nine were to go in her piggy bank.

Last December, Claudia carried the little white box to her first tithing settlement. The bishop handed her a receipt, and we explained to her what it was. She later told her grandmother,

"This paper means I gave Heavenly Father back his money."

Grandmother was so pleased that she opened her handbag and brought forth two nickels. She said, "For a very good little girl."

Claudia took the money to her bedroom. She put one nickel in her piggy bank—and one in her little white box.

Is a child ever too young to be taught the gospel?

Relief Society Magazine, March 1965, p. 217.

ZINA YOUNG CARD
BROWN*

"Mother's Triumph"

Zina was born in 1888. . . . Her father, Charles Ora Card, had been called by John Taylor to establish a colony in southwestern Canada only the year before. The colony that the Cards and fellow Mormons settled came to be known as Cardston, Alberta, Canada.

The home in which Zina was born was a rough log cabin on the main street of the infant settlement of Cardston. "Aunt Zina," as Zina's mother was called by everyone, made the unplastered and unlovely, chinked walls of the cabin into a gracious family home. Zina wrote, "The inside of the cabin was Mother's triumph. She had all the walls and ceilings covered with unbleached muslin. This she in turn covered with colored Canton flannel with the soft, silky nap running down. It was kept

*Zina Young Card Brown was born June 12, 1888, in Cardston, Alberta, Canada. On June 17, 1908, she was married in the Salt Lake Temple to Hugh B. Brown, who has served as an Assistant to the Twelve, a member of the Council of the Twelve, and a member of the First Presidency. They have seven living children, 29 grandchildren, and 51 great-grandchildren. Sister Brown passed away in December 1974. This story appeared in the *New Era*, July 1974, p. 37.

27

looking like satin by frequent stroking with a new broom kept solely for that purpose. These hundreds of yards of Canton were all stitched by Mother on her old treadle sewing machine. Because of her magic touch to the interior of the house, my father called it 'Mother's Canton Flannel Palace.' "

ELLEN R. BRYNER

"An Indian Wail"

It was an early fall morning. The air was crisp and cold. The comforts of the impoverished two rooms of log with earthen floor and roof were very few. Caroline Butler awakened after a night of restless anxiety. There were eleven hungry mouths to feed. For days their rations had been scanty. A little wild game had come to them occasionally from members of the camp, while the husband and father, with his teams and wagons, assisted poorer Saints into Winter Quarters. The food in the larder was not sufficient to satisfy the needs for one meal of the hungry, growing family. As the anxious mother placed the last scanty store of food upon the rough table and urged her family to make preparations for their morning meal, her heart was full of entreaty to God to send help from some source that day.

As they were about to partake, an old Indian woman walked into the room and asked for bread. Caroline was conscious of her family's needs for food and of her own physical weakness from lack of it, because she had given most of her portion to satisfy the hunger of her smaller children. "This is all we have," she answered, "but we will share it with you."

The Indian woman partook and went on her way; not far away through the woods she had thriftily stored some food after the Indian fashion.

Caroline learned that day that bread cast upon the water to satisfy the hungry shall come back a hundredfold. Grandmother Indian (as the old Indian woman was known from that day forth) returned with sufficient dried buffalo meat and dried berries to stay the pangs of hunger until other supplies came. Many times during the Butlers' three years' stay in Winter Quarters, she came to the cabin and shared her own savings of food with her adopted family.

Poverty was the order of the day with these driven and much persecuted Latter-day Saints. As many were doing, this large family was planning the long journey westward without sufficient footwear and clothing, a consequence of the confiscation of their possessions and of being driven from their homes.

Hearing that the journey to the mountains was soon to continue, Grandmother Indian determined to make heavy buckskin moccasins for each member of her adopted family. After tedious weeks of labor, all of the moccasins were finished with the exception of a pair for Caroline. Grandmother Indian spent extra time decorating this pair as a visible sign of her deep devotion. Early one morning, knowing that the time for their departure was near, she approached the little log house only to find her loved ones gone. Almost overcome with disappointment and sorrow, she wailed an Indian wail and started to follow the wagon tracks.

The family traveled five miles that first day. After the campfires had burned low and the oxen were cared for, and all the weary travelers were settled in their beds, an Indian wail was heard in the distance, growing louder as it came nearer. Grandmother Indian had followed her newfound family in order to present her last token of love before a final goodbye. With the moccasins she had brought a generous supply of dried pulverized venison in a pouch, and a sack of dried berries.

INEZ CHANDLER CAGLE*

"I Knew the Lord Would Answer a Mother's Prayer"

In June 1969, my husband, Charles, and I were given a special assignment to attend the organization of the Arkansas Stake. Charles was serving as counselor to the Gulf States Mission president, W. S. Wagstaff, and I was counselor in the mission Relief Society. The Arkansas District, which was part of the Gulf States Mission, was now to become a stake.

On Saturday morning we left our five children in the care of gracious relatives and flew to Little Rock in a small single-engine airplane. At the airport, we met President and Sister Wagstaff and our visiting authorities, Elders Harold B. Lee and James A. Cullimore. Even though clouds began to gather heavily, we anticipated a great spiritual feast and were not disappointed. We attended several inspiring meetings, the last one being the district conference on Sunday when the new stake was formed and the new stake officers were named.

The weather was very bad and my husband had been

---

*Inez Chandler Cagle, a daughter of Nathan Felix and Lillian Sullivan Chandler, was born February 8, 1933, in Winnfield, Louisiana. She was married to Charles Franklin Cagle on January 12, 1951, and they are the parents of five children. Brother Cagle is presently serving as president of the Shreveport Louisiana Stake, and Sister Cagle is a Relief Society teacher and Primary president in her ward.

constantly in touch with the weather advisory station, and their news was always the same—this was a front that had become stationary over the Little Rock area, and there was no chance of it lifting before Tuesday or Wednesday. This was cause for concern to a mother and father who were so far away from their home.

After dinner that evening, President and Sister Wagstaff drove us back to our motel, and when Elder Lee started to get out of the car, I said to him, "Elder Lee, when you say your prayers tonight, I wish you would pray this storm away so we can fly home to our children." He turned to me and said, "Now, Sister Cagle, you go to your room and get a good night's rest. Everything will be all right."

Charles and I went to the Wagstaffs' room and visited until after midnight, discussing the inspiring events of the weekend. When we retired to our room, we made one last call to the weather station at 1:15 A.M. and received the same answer—the storm had settled over the Little Rock area and would not lift before Tuesday or Wednesday. About an hour after we had left Elder Lee, the worst part of the storm had come with crashing thunder, lightning, and heavy rain. Then the weather had seemed to calm, but it continued to rain almost all night.

We awakened early Monday morning and Charles walked outside to check the weather. The rain still dripped off the roof, but the sun was shining brightly and not a cloud was in the sky. We saw Elder Lee walking toward us, smiling, and he remarked, "I knew the Lord would answer a mother's prayer."

You would have to understand the weather in this part of the country to fully appreciate the significance of this event. It is very unusual for a front to stall that far north and then gain enough momentum to carry it out into the Gulf of Mexico that rapidly. As we flew southward toward home, we could see the front rapidly move out into the Gulf.

As we were driving to the airport, I thanked Elder Lee for praying the storm away and he modestly said, "Well, I just reminded Him that he had a concerned mother here who needed to get back to her family."

LUCY GRANT CANNON

"The Will of the Lord"

Faith has always been the fundamental characteristic of Lucy ("Lutie") G. Cannon. From earliest childhood, the Lord has manifested himself in her behalf. When she was about twelve years of age, her mother died. When her father (President Heber J. Grant) told Lucy that her mother was dying, Lucy would not believe him. She hurried from the room and returned with a bottle of consecrated oil and implored him to bless her mother. President Grant blessed his wife, dedicating her to the Lord. As the children left the room, he fell on his knees and prayed that his wife's death might not affect the faith of their children in the ordinances of the gospel. "Lutie" herself ran from the house feeling very bad, as she expressed in the following words:

"I was stunned and shocked and felt my father had not sufficient faith. I went behind the house and knelt down and prayed for the restoration of my mother. Instantly a voice, not an audible one, but one that seemed to speak to my whole being, said, 'In the death of your mother the will of the Lord will be done.' Immediately I was a changed child. I felt reconciled and happy."

Marba C. Josephson, "Careers of Service to Young Womanhood," *Improvement Era*, December 1937, p. 742.

➤ ◆ ➤

33

SARA JANE JENNE CANNON

"Move Away Quickly"

Sara Jane walked every step of the way across the plains except, as she said, "where the streams were too deep to wade."

Once, when she was sent out to gather buffalo chips for the campfires, she was chased by a wild buffalo. She ran toward the encircled wagons in terror and dashed under a wagon just as the head of the animal crashed against the wheel.

Shortly after their arrival in Salt Lake City, her life was saved again by a remarkable warning. She was living with her aunt Jane Richards in an unfinished house with a tarpaulin stretched across the walls for a roof, anchored at each corner with a large boulder. Sara Jane was sitting on a chest against the wall, sewing patchwork, when she heard a voice say, "Move away quickly." There was no one near, but she heeded the warning. Before she had reached the other side of the room, one of the heavy rocks fell, crushing the chest on which she had been sitting.

The early period in Salt Lake was a time of pioneer hardships. In later years Sara Jane seldom talked about the privations or suffering she had borne; but when her daughter Rosannah noticed that she never ate "greens," Sara Jane remarked that she had eaten enough of them in her childhood to last a lifetime.

Beatrice Cannon Evans, *Cannon Family Historical Treasury* (George Cannon Family Association, 1967), p. 124.

ELSIE C. CARROLL

"Snatches of Happiness"

"**M**en are that they might have joy" does not mean that we exist solely to enjoy happiness. Joy does not come to us ready-made as a lasting gift throughout life. Nobody is ever happy twenty-four hours a day, seven days a week. We must learn to snatch happiness in little bits. We must learn to recognize it, or the elements or conditions out of which it can be created, and then form the habit of snatching it and treasuring it while it lasts.

One husband paid his wife the following beautiful tribute: "Mary has the ability to snatch bits of happiness from life as it passes by. Even trying days do not baffle her. Yesterday, when she started to do the weekly washing, something went wrong with the washing machine. She could not get a repairman until the middle of the afternoon. But did she burst into tears or lose her temper? No. Instead, she stirred up a batch of muffins, called a newly made friend with a large family down the street, and told her she was coming to help with a basket of mending she had seen when she and her Relief Society visiting teacher companion had called a few days before. When I came home last night, she did not moan to me about the broken machine or the disruption of the household schedule she likes to keep. She gave me an interesting account of the visit she had had with this overworked neighbor and of plans they had for future working together."

It is worth time and thought to discover sources of happiness within our reach and the possibilities we have of taking advantage of them. We may not be able to travel to different parts of the world, to attend fine operas and stimulating lectures, to wear costly clothes, or live in elegant homes, but we can thrill over the grandeur in nature, we can read good books, we can make family relationships joyous and precious, and we can be gladdened by the opportunities and blessings of friendships. And, above all, we can find enduring joy in staying close to our Father in heaven.

Relief Society Magazine, July 1965, p. 514.

HANNAH CHRISTINA CHALARSON

"An Apostle of the Lord"

The following story was written by Hannah Christina Chalarson's son

My mother, Hannah Christina Bjorkman, was born in Malmaland, Sweden, on October 22, 1850. She was reared in the Lutheran faith until she was twenty-six years old, when she met the Latter-day Saint missionaries, heard their message, and was converted and joined the Church.

Her family, friends, and even her sweetheart turned against her; she was cast out and disowned.

In 1880 she immigrated to the United States and went to Utah. She met and married Hans Nadrian Chalarson in January 1884. Two children were born to this union, Frank on December 26, 1884, and Albert on October 29, 1886. In 1886 they went to Arizona, where my father engaged in farming for a time; then he went into the sawmill business.

She was a Relief Society teacher and attended Relief Society regularly. She never heard from her folks or friends. She passed away at my home in Tempe, Arizona, on December 7, 1932, at the age of 82. We laid her to rest at Thatcher.

When I was a young man, we lived close to President Andrew Kimball, Spencer W. Kimball's father. My mother and I were coming home one evening just about dark. Spencer was milking the cows and singing at the top of his voice. My mother stopped dead still for a few seconds and then said, "That boy will one day be an apostle of the Lord." We walked perhaps twenty feet farther and she stopped again. This time she seemed to be out of breath. She raised both her hands and looked up and said, "Yes! And he might even live to lead this church."

Roberta Flake Clayton, comp., *Pioneer Women of Arizona* (Mesa, Arizona, 1969), pp. 76-77.

VIRGINIA DRIGGS CLARK

"Blessings in Disguise"

I have had an experience that I think others might like to hear. It was mine to have—but not mine to keep.

Two months before our baby boy was born, the doctors found it necessary for me to have a major operation for cancer. During the time of my convalescence and while we awaited the arrival of the baby, we had frequent prayers. The stake, under the leadership of President Ezra Taft Benson, united in fasting and prayer. I was administered to often; and many, many times the voices of our three children (the baby could not talk) were raised in the petition, "Help Mother to get well soon." The doctors shook their heads. I had one chance in one thousand—it was only a question of time.

What I want others to know is the experience that came because of this illness. The spirit of humility was poured down upon us, and the knowledge that God is all-powerful was made known to us. Through frequent prayers, we were led to trust in his plan and to know that all would be well.

The spirit of repentance permeated our home. We felt that we must live better and do better if we would expect the Lord to bless us and give us what we wanted so very much.

The spirit of our love toward each other and our children,

and of the children toward each other, was felt. We showed each other every day the affection and appreciation we had for each other. Days might be numbered, but love would guide us through.

The spirit of appreciation for our blessings came to us, and we felt as if our cup would run over. Our little boy was born and was perfect. The children remained well. My husband, Harold, was blessed with health to carry on his work and church activities. Life took on new meanings. God had been good to us.

And there came to us a display of friendliness. A neighbor across the alley, whose antagonism against anyone who would have so many children in the city had made little unpleasantries on various occasions, sent with the children large bouquets of flowers that she had grown and picked from her own garden; and for the first time in the year we had lived there, she smiled and waved to me.

There came to us gifts of all kinds—flowers, food, and clothes. Money came to us through the mail with the simple greeting, "Merry Christmas." Interested friends who knew we had not been able to can during the summer brought to us over a hundred quarts of fruits and vegetables. A young lady who had never met me knitted a wool sweater for the baby.

Blessings came to us because Harold continued in his calling as a bishop. When asked about financial arrangements, the doctors said, "You're a bishop in your church. We will give you service at a minimum charge."

When I returned to the hospital for the second time for an operation, there was no one to care for the family. A young lady who was visiting her sister volunteered to come into our home. She had never met us, but for two weeks she had complete charge of five children and the house. When she was ready to return to her family we gave her a little gift and hid some money in the package—money that we knew she would not accept outright. The next day she came back with it, and with tears in her eyes she said, "It has been an honor for me to be in the home of the bishop. My husband is in the South Pacific, and I do not want to be deprived of any blessings by taking pay. I know that my reward will come in other ways." She would not accept any remuneration.

People say to me, "Oh, how terrible! What an awful experience your sickness has been. You must try to forget it and start a new life."

It must not be that way! I never want to forget. And so I put these things down in writing that I may remember. I know that the memory of it will make me a happier and better person.

Instructor, September 1960, p. 297.

GENEVA RACHEL CLIFF

"Ride into the Sun"

As told by Nora Eddington°

The ninth grade commercial arithmetic class at Wasatch High School in Heber City, Utah, had a new pupil. Ordinarily such an occasion produced swift but rapidly diminishing interest. But an incoming ninth grader was not ordinarily thirty-four years old, nor did she weigh a generous 200 pounds. Little wonder that Geneva's agonizing efforts to fit such bulk beneath a child-size school desk produced general and wide-eyed astonishment.

At the death of her husband, Geneva Rachel Cliff received a legacy that listed (on the debit side) seven children, staggering hospital and medical bills, a year's accumulation of unpaid grocery slips, and a large frame dwelling replete with missing doorknobs, peeling paint, and worn-out furnishings, surrounded by a tumbledown fence. To further complicate the widow's position, America was in the midst of the greatest depression in its history.

Sister Cliff's assets included a tiny insurance benefit, borrowed against in times of family crises almost to the point of nonexistence, her dead husband's inspirational example of moral

° Nora Eddington is a free-lance writer, an executive secretary, a homemaker, and the mother of two sons and three daughters. She is a member of the Murray Twelfth Ward, Murray Utah Stake, and has served in many ward capacities.

and physical courage despite bodily deterioration and economic adversity, and a great love for and faith in her Heavenly Father.

That first lonely summer of her widowhood, Geneva Cliff plied every skill she knew, with little success, in an attempt to wrest a livelihood for her family. Then, with courage born of desperation, she entered local politics. November found her duly elected county treasurer, a position she was to fill with great efficiency for twelve years.

Thus it was that Geneva Rachel Cliff enrolled for formal high school training in typing, English, bookkeeping, and commercial arithmetic. She must, of necessity, master these skills in the period from November to January, at which time her duties as county treasurer would begin.

But fresh adversity overshadowed her triumph at the polls. At a time when she needed almost superhuman physical health to wrestle with her problems, she developed arthritis and was deprived of the use of her legs. Between home and office the Cliff children pulled their mother on the family sled.

Near the Wasatch County Courthouse stood the local jail. An upper courthouse room served for detention of minors who had transgressed the law. Most of the young offenders were starved for affection, understanding, and help. With eventual hard-won mobility, Geneva Cliff took it upon herself to supply this lack. Each new occupant detained by the law was visited and received gifts of comfort, love, and common-sense advice, plus Geneva's home-baked treats.

Learning of a state program to aid the handicapped, Geneva ferreted out all such hapless individuals in the community and assisted them in making the necessary application for assistance. Into an already bulging house came waifs in need of mothering. Homeless girls with unwanted babies were furnished shelter and care until proper provision could be made for their welfare. Like homing pigeons, down-on-their-luck transients haunted her door, confident of a hot, nourishing meal.

Geneva's unmatched sense of humor and hearty laugh helped to sustain her brood. The face of trouble was never dissolved by tears, she insisted, but only worsened with a headache.

Not the smallest pittance could be spared for personal pleasure. Knowing this, and aware of the widow's boundless enthusiasm for Will Rogers, the local movie proprietor sent Sister

Cliff a ticket for each film featuring the homespun philosopher. This kindly gesture paid dividends, the movie manager claimed. Fully as many patrons attended the theater to share Geneva's unrestrained laughter as came to view the film.

First, a new fence around two acres necessitated the removal of several large trees. With the trees felled, it was up to the children to saw the wood into lengths and split it for furnace fuel. Each morning and evening the three oldest, assisting each other, sawed off two lengths apiece; then Geneva sawed one length with each of them. A furnace consumes many tons of fuel during a northern Utah winter, and eventually the trees were disposed of. The task of supplying the black monster's insatiable appetite was then assigned to the four younger children, who had to haul countless tubs of twigs and chips into the house if they were to keep warm.

Though deeply sympathetic to their complaints of frustration and fatigue, this wise mother accomplished her purpose. She taught her children the value of work, conserved costly fuel, disposed of unsightly debris, and kept her youngsters too busy to find mischief while she was away at work.

Next came the gigantic task of home remodeling. Geneva tore plaster from cracked walls and hauled it away in a wheelbarrow. She brought petrified wood a distance of six miles, in any sort of vehicle that could be commandeered, for a chimney and fireplace mantel. Aided only by the older children, she dug a cesspool and basement stair excavation and painted to glistening whiteness the entire structure.

The garden was a difficult but glorious task. Again the trusty wheelbarrow came into play as Geneva hauled tons of dirt for new walks, lawns, and flower beds. Eventually her garden boasted 195 varieties of flowers, not including variations of some species, their beauty and fragrance answering a mother's love for beauty.

Only in the solitude of her own bedroom, with seven children safely asleep, did she give vent to her loneliness and her fear for the family's future. The Lord received her petitions and strengthened her for each new day.

Despising the weedy unkemptness that often goes with small towns, Geneva began planting flowers on ditchbanks and along roadsides. She organized the first flower club in Wasatch County. This led to the organization of clubs in other towns. She gave twenty-five dollars of her own money as a prize for the best flower garden and donated seeds and tubs of plants to all who requested them.

School and other public grounds that had once been full of weeds or used for pasture were assigned to the garden club as a community project, with Sister Cliff personally supervising planting of lawns and shrubs. She visited the superintendent of a nearby mine with a request for old pipe, which was cut and welded for fences, then painted. Inspired by the beauty already accomplished, Heber City fathers now came forward with additional funds and enthusiastic help.

For her outstanding contributions Geneva Cliff was listed in *Who's Who in American Government*. She also became the only female member of the Heber City Chamber of Commerce.

A Boy Scout troop was headquartered in an upper room of the Cliff home. An Indian-head plaque decorated the door of this special sanctuary. Here a troubled boy could bring his problems, warmed by the complete assurance of a confidential reception, a sympathetic ear, and wise counsel. Within the framework of the Church this amazing mother organized young boys for competitive sports, including marble tournaments.

The Cliff children were surrounded by beauty and were taught to appreciate it. Every child had an opportunity to study music and have his own instrument. Their collection included a piano, bass horn, baritone horn, cornet, mandolin, violin, and oboe.

During this period the local high school band placed first in the state competition but lost national recognition because of lack of instrumentation. To the rescue came Geneva Cliff. She organized a band sponsors' club to procure new instruments and uniforms. Subsequently this small high school took three successive first place awards in its own division, then challenged larger schools and won three more such standings.

"Mama was a strong character," the oldest daughter relates, "and an individualist. What other people might say or think of her activities or the way she dressed, lived, or spent her paycheck never bothered her in the least as long as she knew her goal was a worthy one.

"Her goals were definite: to be able to meet Papa on his own intellectual plane so he needn't be ashamed of her; to rear and educate her family to be self-dependent and to appreciate life; to have no ill will among family members, friends or the community; to burden no other individual with her problems; and to serve an honorable mission for her church."

All these goals Geneva Rachel Cliff successfully attained. After her children were grown, she attended college for various periods, then accepted a missionary call to the Western Canadian Mission. She died three months after entering the mission field.

Greek mythology records the story of a horse no man could ride. Finally came one who persevered until he successfully accomplished the feat. Asked the secret of his success, the rider modestly stated that he noticed how fearful the animal was of its own shadow. "As long as I rode him into the sun," he said, "I was successful."

"Ride into the sun!" Upon such philosophy Geneva Cliff reared her family, teaching by precept and example that one sees shadows only when he takes his eyes from his goal.

Ensign, August 1972, pp. 87-89.

Biographical Sketch

HANNAH CORNABY

Hannah Cornaby was born March 17, 1822, near Beccles, Suffolk, England, the eldest child of William and Hannah Hollingsworth Last. On January 30, 1851, she was married to Samuel Cornaby, and the following year they were converted to the Church. They sailed for America January 9, 1853, traveling by way of New Orleans and St. Louis to Keokuk, Iowa. From there they traveled by ox team and wagon on to Salt Lake City.

Three years after their arrival in Salt Lake City, the Cornabys moved to Spanish Fork, where they reared their family. Sister Cornaby, an active worker in the Relief Society, wrote numerous poems, one of which, "Who's on the Lord's Side, Who?" has been a popular hymn of the Saints. In 1881 she published a book titled *Autobiography and Poems*. In it she described her arrival in the Salt Lake Valley:

When at length, from the top of the Little Mountain, we caught a first glimpse of the 'Valley,' our delight and gratitude found vent in tears of unfeigned joy, and when, on the morning of the 12th of October, 1853, we emerged from the mouth of Emigration Canyon and beheld the 'City of the Saints,' we felt more than repaid for the nine months of travel, and all the hardships we had endured. We seemed to inhale the restful spirit of the beautiful city, spread out in peaceful loveliness before us. The neat adobe houses with their trim gardens, the crystal streams coursing along the sidewalks, giving life to avenues of shade trees, all aglow with the lovely tints of autumn, presented a picture that is indelibly fixed upon our minds. . . .

From her poems we read:

The prayer is breathed that on each path
    truth's own pure light may shine.
Brightening the sombre hues of earth
    with radiance divine.
Onward and upward clear and bright
    may it direct our course
Back to the fountainhead of light,
    its own eternal source.

She died in Spanish Fork, Utah, on September 1, 1905.

HANNAH CORNABY

I was early taught by my parents to love that Being, who has made the earth so beautiful, and who has provided so much for his creatures dwelling thereon; thus I was early led to admire and reverence the Creator through his works; and especially from my mother's teaching, I learned my duty to him, as revealed in the Bible. This sacred book was my mother's companion by day and by night; and before I was able to read, I had committed to memory, under her tuition, many of its holy precepts. When, at six years of age, I began to trace the simpler portions myself, I knew no greater enjoyment than reading its pages, and I committed to memory much of the New Testament and the Psalms.

When I was about seven years of age, the most wonderful and venerated event of my life occurred, although I cannot recollect the exact date thereof. I have never written an account of this circumstance, realizing that no language of mine could adequately describe it; and now, after a period of fifty years, a feeling of awe comes over me, which I try in vain to overcome.

My father and I were walking in our garden one evening, in the mellow twilight, and a quiet gray beauty pervaded the scene, when a sudden flash of light made us start; and turning toward the point whence it proceeded, we saw a remarkable streak of red, rising in the west, which captured our attention by its brightness. While watching its upward course, an arm, and a hand holding a roll were plainly visible; and soon the form of a person appeared, full in sight, following the streak of red before mentioned. A light, similar to the first, followed this wonderful personage, and the whole procession slowly moved through the midst of the heavens, then disappeared at the eastern boundary of the horizon. During the passage of this heavenly being across the entire arch of the sky, the right hand was in motion, waving the roll, as if showing it to the inhabitants of the earth. This wonderful vision having disappeared, my father and I, hand in hand, stood as if spellbound, when we heard two men passing along the road (from which a living fence of hedge separated us) discoursing on what they, as well as ourselves, had seen. The one remarked to the other that he thought it could not be an angel, as no wings were visible; we, too, had observed this, yet believed it to be an angel. A loose robe covered the body, leaving the arms and a portion of the limbs visible.

As soon as we were able to walk, we went to the house. Mother saw that something unusual had happened and asked what made us so pale. At my request, Father allowed me to relate to her what we had seen. When I had given an account of this strange phenomenon, she was much affected and remarked that it was one of the signs of the last days, which, according to the Revelations of St. John, would transpire.

I had loved God before; now I feared and reverenced him and desired to know more of that Being who rules in the heavens above and on the earth beneath. I loved to be alone, especially at eventide, to watch the heavens, thinking another angel would appear.

Hannah Cornaby, *Autobiography and Poems* (Salt Lake City: J.C. Graham & Co., 1881), pp. 9-12.

"That Is Your Future Husband"

"Suitors came, my hand to claim," but as yet my heart gave no response to this symphony of love, although I appreciated the honor they sought to confer on me. My friends blamed me, and predicted for me the fate of an old maid. This, however, did not distress me, for my Bible said, "Be not unequally yoked with unbelievers," and, thinking myself a believer, I feared to be yoked with an unbeliever. None of those who had presented themselves had made any profession of religion.

But a day came when, as in all my life, I had been "led in a way I knew not"; so, with this important step it was the same.

One day I was in the town on business, walking along Market Street, intent only on the errand which called me there, when I passed a young man, an entire stranger to me. Now there was nothing remarkable in the appearance of this stranger, but something whispered, "That is your future husband." Surprised at this, I turned to take a look at him, and, to my annoyance, he had also turned to look at me. Ashamed of myself for this breach of street etiquette, I hastily resumed my way, and this stranger who had thus attracted my attention was lost to sight. Not so with the interest he had created in my heart. Business was for the time forgotten; I walked aimlessly on, thinking of this strange event, when I was met by my sister Amelia, who asked what had happened to make me look so pleased. I told her frankly of the singular circumstance just recorded. She smiled and said, "Oh, my romantic sister." I replied, "Do not make fun of me; I shall marry that man, or I shall never marry on this earth."

Months rolled on. I could not drive from my thoughts this singular incident, when, apparently by the merest accident, at the house of a friend, I met and was introduced to a Mr. Cornaby, who had come to Beccles to take charge of a public school. Here, dear reader, let me introduce to you my future husband; for in this gentleman I recognized the mysterious stranger who for months had filled my thoughts. Though perturbed and agitated, I concealed my emotion and left the house as quickly as possible; and in the quietude of my own room, I thought and prayed earnestly for the guidance of the Holy Spirit to direct me aright. Accidental meetings with Mr. Cornaby, friendship. . . .

And on January 30th, 1851, we were married in St. George's Church, a venerable structure, celebrated for its antiquity and architectural beauty.

Autobiography and Poems, pp. 17-21.

<hr />

HANNAH CORNABY

"Fear Not, for I Am with Thee"

Among the current literature of the day that, in the way of business, passed through the bookstore that we owned, was a series of tracts published by Chambers, one of which, entitled "Religious Impostors," attracted our attention. After giving an account of various religious impostors, it concluded by giving a brief history of Joseph Smith; a footnote on the last page stated that the editors had heard, since the pamphlet had gone to press, that Joseph Smith had been killed by a mob. They regretted to hear this, for the reason that his fanatical followers would regard him as a martyr, and the delusion would spread.

This was our first introduction to Mormonism. Soon after this, another book came our way, entitled *The Mormons, Illustrated*, published by the Illustrated London News Company. It contained copious extracts from Colonel Kane's lectures before the Historical Society of Pennsylvania; also some of Joseph Smith's teachings. Although the book was written to show the fallacy of "Mormonism," it made a deep impression on my mind. My husband and I read it together carefully and thoughtfully, and we arose from our reading satisfied of the divine mission of Joseph Smith. . . .

We often took long walks by the seaside, unseen save by that eye that is ever over the righteous, and prayed and talked upon the subject that occupied so much of our thoughts. This struggle went on for months. . . .

It was the beginning of February 1852, on a cold stormy evening, that, looking out at the door to watch the progress of the storm, I saw a man sheltering under the awning in front of our store. I invited him to come inside for better protection from the weather. This he did, expressing his thanks, but he assured me that if I knew who he was, I probably would not welcome him under my roof. I was startled at this but replied that I had only done what was my duty to any fellow creature under the circumstances.

He then introduced himself as George Day, a Latter-day Saint elder, who had been sent to preach the gospel in that town. I remarked that I thought we had ministers enough already to preach the gospel, to which he replied that none of them had authority to preach, but he had been sent with authority as the Savior had sent his disciples. I then hastened to call my husband, who received him courteously and invited him to supper. After supper he spent the evening with us, telling of the latter-day work; we listened with great interest until bedtime. We procured lodging for him at a hotel nearby, and he breakfasted with us next morning. Before he left, he made an appointment, at our request, to call again that evening and preach to us, we promising to call in our near neighbors to hear him.

Evening came, and with it Elder Day and the friends we had invited. He preached and we believed, and thought it impossible for anyone who heard it to do otherwise; but with our neighbors, it was different. They could scarcely refrain from abusing him and us, and called us fools for listening to such lies. We were astonished beyond measure at this, thinking they would be so glad; but we were too happy to be angry at such strange conduct. When Elder Day left, we gave him permission to make our house his home when he had no other.

This meeting caused a great hue and cry, with parsons and others coming to hear about this new religion. We could do little else than answer questions. It was such a sudden turn of affairs, we hardly knew what to do—our friends became enemies and we were persecuted and annoyed in many ways. Before this, we had been respected and esteemed by many. Now, if we walked along the streets, we met no kindly greeting, but were pointed out as "Saints," and sometimes stoned.

Others believed us, though, and a few were baptized when Elder Claudius V. Spencer, then president of the Norwich Conference, came and organized a branch of The Church of Jesus Christ of Latter-day Saints in the town of Great Yarmouth. Elder Spencer removed a few lingering doubts from my husband's mind, and he was baptized and confirmed.

I too desired baptism, but the birth of our first child delayed it for a time. We placed the publications of the Church in our store windows. These attracted considerable attention and at the same time relieved us from answering so many questions. As soon as my health would permit, I renewed my request for baptism. A time was appointed to attend to this ordinance. I left my babe in the care of a nurse whom I could trust, and proceeded to a house near the seaside, where we met to make preparations.

We found the house surrounded by a mob, through which we made our way with difficulty, amid oaths and threats of what would be done if any attempt were made to go into the water. We waited until near midnight, hoping the crowd would disperse; but it had all this time been increasing, until it numbered many hundreds. We feared violence, not only to ourselves but to the family under whose roof we were waiting.

Wearied of the delay, the master of the house thought of a ruse. He went to the door and asked permission for his son to pass through the crowd to his boat, as he was a fisherman, and it was necessary that he should sail with the outgoing tide. My husband, previously dressed in the son's clothes, stepped out, and I followed, unnoticed, in the darkness. The mob soon discovered that their prey had escaped, and before we reached the water's edge, the whole horde was upon us. My husband baptized me amid a shower of stones and shouts of "Duck him! Duck him!" and other such cries. Elder Day appealed for protection to the police, several of whom were present, but they said they could do nothing.

We then made our way back, as best we could, followed by the mob. Although the stones whizzed around us as thick as hail, not one touched us, and we reached home in safety, thanking God for our miraculous deliverance and determined, more than ever, with the assistance of the Holy Spirit, to adhere to the principles we had embraced. At the next meeting of the Saints, I was confirmed, and I knew for myself that the work was of God.

Although persecution continued, many attended our meetings, and a few were added to the Church, until our branch numbered twenty-seven members.

Autobiography and Poems, pp. 21-25.

<hr/>

HANNAH CORNABY

"Gathering Flowers"

Many of the Saints in the Norwich Conference were expecting to go to the "Valley" the approaching season. We too had caught the spirit of gathering and felt that England was no longer our home.

On the ninth day of January, 1853, we left Norwich, after a stay of only seven months, during which time we witnessed a great outpouring of the Spirit of God on priesthood and members, young and old. We had seen a miraculous display of the signs following those who believed; we had heard speaking in tongues and the interpretation of the same; we had seen the sick instantly healed and evil spirits cast out. We heard the brethren and sisters testify to the truth of the latter-day work, and we took with us assurances of its truth that intervening years have not effaced. . . .

Inseparably connected with this happy time were the occasions when we were guests under the hospital roof of Mother Teasdel and her son, Brother Samuel P., listening while Sister

Teasdel told, among other incidents connected with the commencement of the latter-day work in Norwich, of a dream in which she saw the man who would first bring the gospel to Norwich; and how, long afterwards, she saw and recognized the same man on the street, in the person of Elder Thomas Smith; and, as directed by the Spirit, accosted the stranger, telling him of her dream and inviting him to her house, thus being the first to open her house to a Latter-day Saint elder in the Norwich Conference. . . .

We proceeded from St. Louis to Keokuk on the steamer *Kate Kearney;* arriving there late in the day, we were obliged to shelter for the night in a large warehouse on the levee, without any accommodation but that afforded by our luggage.

Next morning, we proceeded to our camp on the brow of a hill overlooking the Mississippi River. Here we found our wagons and tents. We had just placed our baggage in the wagons. Some people were making awkward attempts at erecting tents while others were trying to place the covers on the wagons, some of which obstinately refused to reach over at both ends, when we were struck by a furious storm of wind and rain, accompanied by thunder and lightning such as we had never heard or seen before. The storm raged with such fury that we feared the wagons would be upset, and after the wind had subsided, the rain poured down incessantly three days and nights, our luggage and bedding becoming thoroughly soaked and the campground ankle deep with mud. Under these circumstances, my second child was prematurely born. A serious illness followed, but through the mercy of God and the tender care of my husband, I recovered.

During our stay there of one month, awaiting the arrival of the oxen and cows for our journey, we became somewhat familiarized with camp life. Our introductory storm having ceased and our clothes and bedding dried, we enjoyed the genial sunshine and the beauties of nature. The surrounding country was delightful in the habiliments of spring. Wildflowers of great beauty and variety were profuse in the woods. Many of the brethren obtained employment. Our Scandinavian brethren, with characteristic industry and forethought, purchased trees from the owners of the neighboring forests, from which they manufactured a variety of useful articles. Time passed swiftly. All were busy preparing for the journey.

It was three years to a day, from that memorable first of June before mentioned, that we left Keokuk. I wish I could afford a page to a description of our starting. The oxen were wild, and getting them yoked was the most laughable sight I had ever witnessed; everybody was giving orders, and nobody knew how to carry them out. If the men had not been Saints, there would doubtless have been much profane language used; but the oxen, not understanding "English" anyway, did just as well without it. But it did seem so truly comical to witness the bewildered look of some innocent brother who, after having labored an hour or more to get "Bright" secured to one end of the yoke, would hold the other end aloft trying to persuade "Buck" to come under, only to see "Bright" careening across the countryside, the yoke lashing the air, and he not even giving a hint as to when he intended to stop.

Through the previous exertions and skill of our never-to-be-forgotten friend William B. Woods, our team was made somewhat tractable; it was finally hitched up for the start. . . .

We were enabled, by selling some of our surplus clothing, to provide ourselves with many little comforts, and even what were then considered luxuries. Among other things, we purchased a good supply of groceries, an extra tent, and some cooking utensils, also a lamp and oil, which we used to good advantage when the train halted a few days for repairs, etc. My husband also procured a good outfit of fishing tackle, and being an expert angler, supplied our table with wholesome fish. By a little forethought and management, the daily routine of camp life was by no means irksome. I often think that the weeks spent crossing the plains were as full of instruction and interest as any part of our lives. We had abundant opportunities to behold nature and its varied beauties. Especially did we admire the flowers—growing in some places in great profusion—handfuls of which daily adorned the wagon and delighted our child, who was in the care of a sister who was too feeble to walk. The delicious wild fruits seen at different stages of the journey were much relished and afforded a wholesome variety to our diet.

In consequence of the wagons being heavily loaded, all who were able had to walk. It was a very interesting sight each morning to see our company break camp; the long train of wagons would stretch itself out like a huge snake and then begin to wind along the boundless prairies. Those on foot ahead of the train presented a motley appearance in their travel-worn dress, walking in groups, chatting, singing, laughing, talking principles and politics, or passing jokes, as the case might be, all care being left behind. Some might be seen rambling on the prairies gathering flowers, others picking berries. . . .

After supper, groups could be seen around the campfires, singing the songs of Zion, talking of bygone days or the hopes of the future, until the bugle call for prayers, when all except the guards (for we watched as well as prayed) retired to rest.

Autobiography and Poems, pp. 28-34.

HANNAH CORNABY

"A Loaf of Bread in Payment"

It was evening. I was just preparing the little ones for bed when my daughter Edith asked what we should do for breakfast. I told her not to think about breakfast, as she had had supper and was not hungry then; but *she* reasoned that we had better tell the Lord that we had nothing for breakfast.

So, kneeling down with the children, one on either side of me, I told our Father what we needed. Afterward, I was putting them to bed when a knock summoned me to the door. A neighbor came in with a large parcel in her arms and said that she wanted to write a letter to her husband, then on a mission to the Sandwich Islands; not having writing materials, she had come to see if I could supply her with some and offered, with apologies, a loaf of bread in payment. I supplied her with what she wanted, and she departed, satisfied and pleased, leaving me more thankful than words can describe.

Oh, what a loaf of bread that was, so large and light! The joy of the dear children knew no bounds. We thanked God, knowing that for many days we should not be hungry.

Autobiography and Poems, p. 41.

◆━━━◆

HANNAH CORNABY

"What a Dinner We Had That Day"

I trust to be forgiven for adding another circumstance to that just related. One morning having, as usual, attended to family prayer, in which, with greater significance than is often used, we asked, "Give us this day our daily bread," and having eaten a rather scanty breakfast—every morsel we had in the house—Edith was wondering what we should have for dinner and why Pa had not sent us some fish. I too was anxious, not having heard from Provo for some days; so, telling my darling I would go and see if Sister Ellen Jackson (whose husband was also one of the fishing party) had heard any news, I started off. Sister Jackson had not heard from the fishery but was quite cheerful, telling me how well her garden was growing, adding that the radishes were fit for use, and insisting that I must have some. It was good to see something to eat; and, quite pleased, I bade her good morning. I passed on my way the house of Brother Charles Gray, and Sister Gray asked me where I had gotten such fine radishes. I told her and offered to divide them with her, to which she agreed, providing I would take in exchange some lettuce and cress, of which she had plenty. She filled a pan with these, and I hurried away thinking how pleased my children would be, if only we had bread to eat with them.

As I was passing Brother Simon Baker's house, Sister Baker saw me and invited me in. I told her I had left my children and could not stop long. She then asked me where I had gotten such nice green stuff, and when I told her and offered her some, she replied, "If I could exchange some for butter, I would be glad." She then gave me a piece of nice fresh butter, which had just come from their dairy on the Jordan, and also a large slice of cheese. If I only had bread, I thought, how good these would be! Just then my eyes rested upon a large vessel full of broken bread. Sister Baker, seeing I had noticed it, told me its history. It had been sent the day before, in a sack, to the canyon where her husband had a number of men working. On the way it had fallen from the wagon and been crushed under the wheel. She did not know what to do with it, remarking that she would offer me some of it but feared I would feel insulted, although she assured me it was perfectly clean. I accepted her offer, and, after filling a large pan, she sent her daughter home with me to carry it.

The children were watching for my return, and when they saw the bread, they clapped their hands with delight. Bread, butter, cheese, radishes, lettuce, and cress! What a dinner we had that day! Elijah never enjoyed the dinner the ravens brought him more than I did that meal; nor did he more fully understand that a kind Providence had furnished it.

Autobiography and Poems, pp. 41-42.

◄──►

HANNAH CORNABY

"Gingerbread Toys"

The recent famine experience had taught me economy, and the little I could procure from the sale of some clothing enabled us to live. I could have made our condition known and have received help, but delicacy forbade; so I made the best of the situation, exerting myself unceasingly for the helpless little ones.

Christmas Eve came, and my darlings, with childish faith, hung up their stockings, wondering if Santa Claus would fill them. With aching heart, which I concealed from them, I assured them they would not be forgotten; and they fell asleep with joyful anticipation for the morrow.

Not having a particle of sweetening, I knew not what to do. They must not, however, be disappointed. I then thought of some squashes in the house, which I boiled, then strained off the liquid; that, when simmered a few hours, made a sweet syrup. With this and a little spice, I made gingerbread dough which, when cut into every conceivable variety of design and baked in a skillet (I had no stove), filled their stockings and pleased them as much as would the most fancy confectionaries.

I sometimes wonder if the children of today enjoy the costly Christmas presents of toys and rich candies with which they are surfeited any more than my little ones did their gingerbread toys.

Autobiography and Poems, pp. 45-46.

➤◆➤

HANNAH CORNABY

"Point of the Mountain"

In a few weeks, my husband started for Spanish Fork to seek a new home, having heard while in Provo of the advantages it offered to new settlers—namely, plenty of land with a good supply of water. This was in August 1856.

We rented a house, purchased a good building site, and built a small room in which to winter. This had just been accomplished when my husband was taken very sick, but he recovered in a month sufficiently to take a journey to Salt Lake City on business. He had just reached his destination when unfortunately he took a heavy chill and became entirely prostrated by rheumatic and lung fever.

At this time I received a letter from a friend in Salt Lake City, informing me that if I wished to see my husband alive, I must go to him at once; but the difficulties in the way seemed almost insurmountable. The roads were nearly impassable for snow. I was sixty miles from Salt Lake City.

On the third day of January, 1847, the teams started for Salt Lake City, and I with them; I had arranged to leave my two eldest children in the care of Sister Isabella Rockhill. The first day we traveled twelve miles, reaching Provo at dark. Greatly to my surprise, I met Brother John B. Milner, with whom we had become acquainted in crossing the ocean on board the *Ellen Marie*. He, with his wife, made me welcome for the night, offering the best accommodation their house afforded. The following night I spent at Lehi, at the house of Elder Robert Winter, my husband's brother-in-law, who accompanied me the next day on the journey.

I must mention a very providential deliverance I had that day. We had to pass what is known as the "Point of the Mountain," the divide separating Utah and Salt Lake valleys. The ascending grade made it impossible for the teams, six in number, to travel without doubling. This slow operation rendered it very tedious sitting so long in the wagon; and I became so benumbed that, following the advice of the teamster, I dismounted and walked on, with my babe well wrapt. The piercing wind and blinding snow made it hard work to keep moving, yet necessity compelled me to walk fast to keep from freezing. This took me so far ahead of the teams that suddenly I realized I was lost. I attempted to retrace my steps but was met by the wind and drifting snow, which I could not face; but I continued on. At length I became so exhausted, I thought I must sit down; but knowing this would mean death, I prayed to God for help and then waded through snow, drifted so deep in some places that it was impossible to trace the road. Stupefied and benumbed as I was, I wandered into a ravine, sinking down into a deep snowdrift, which nearly covered me.

I had just enough consciousness to wonder whether my babe was alive, and how long it would be until the teams would find me, when a stupor came over me, from which I was aroused by a kindly voice. Looking up, I saw a horse's head quite close. A man passing with a sleigh had seen me and was trying to lift me out, yet feared his assistance had come to late. He helped me into the sleigh and drove to a house about two miles distant. By the time the teams came up, I had quite recovered. My babe was in deep sleep and had not suffered.

We stayed at Draperville that night. Next day, Mr. Winter went ahead of the teams to inform my husband of my coming and then sent a sleigh to meet me.

I found my husband very sick, but the worst was over; and in six weeks from that time he was sufficiently convalescent to return. On reaching home, we found the children all right. They had been well cared for in our absence.

Spring had set in; my husband, as soon as he was able, taught the ward school; and we spent the summer very comfortably and began to enjoy country life.

Autobiography and Poems, pp. 43-49.

---◆---

HANNAH CORNABY

"I Felt the Healing Power"

On the 14th of November, 1863, another daughter was born to us. She was a fine healthy babe, and no words could describe the joy of our household at this event.

Not being able to attend fast meeting, Bishop Thurber and other elders came to my house, and we named our treasure Grace Emily Lydia. We called her Grace, as no other name seemed so suited to our darling.

In September, when she was ten months old, she was suddenly taken very sick. We called in the elders and administered mild herbs according to the Word of Wisdom, but all in vain. Our Grace faded away like a sweet autumn flower touched by the hand of death.

On the 27th of October, 1864, she was taken from us. Like David of old, while she was sick we wept and fasted and prayed; but after she was gone, like him, we reasoned, we shall go to her, but she cannot return to us. We resolved not to displease our Father in heaven by pining over this loss, so we set to work to gather up the broken threads of life and to provide for the comfort of the dear ones still left with us.

A week after her death, and while diligently employed, I was suddenly prostrated by sickness, the like of which I had never known. At first we hoped it was only from the heavy strain my system had lately endured, and would soon pass off. We did all that wisdom dictated, all that the love and affection of my family and friends could devise, yet with but short intervals, this debility and weakness lasted nearly six years.

I felt very feeble in body and depressed in mind when Brother William H. Darger, our block teacher, came to administer the sacrament to me. He noticed that I was not as well as usual and asked if I wished to be administered to before he left. My husband anointed my head with consecrated oil, after which they placed their hands upon my head and blessed me.

In an instant I felt the healing power in every part of my body. Several persons present at the time also testified to the power that attended the words.

When Brother Darger was leaving, he said, "You will soon be well." I replied that I knew I would. Both my daughters told me they felt that the time for my recovery had come. I did not say much; I was so astonished at this wonderful event that I seemed overpowered by the greatness of the blessing that had come upon me.

Next morning, when alone with my daughter Mary, I told her I was well, and requested her to bring my clothes so I might dress and arise from my bed. She wished me to wait until her father came in, but I wanted no one except her with me. I then got out of bed and, with one hand laid upon her shoulder, walked six times the length of the bed. My darling child was so overjoyed that she exclaimed with uplifted hands, "Oh, Mother, give the glory to God, give all the glory to him, for it is all his work!" and she wept for joy. My husband came in at the time, was astonished, and joined us in thanksgiving to God.

Autobiography and Poems, pp. 52-53, 58.

———◆——◆———

HANNAH CORNABY

"No, a Thousand Times, No"

It is more than six years since I was healed by the power of God; and if not robust, my health has been measurably good, enabling me to some extent to attend to my domestic duties, and in the summertime to enjoy myself in the cultivation of flowers, raising silk, and assisting in our apiary. Although not able to take an active part in public life, I have attended meetings occasionally and have spoken of "the goodness of God in the congregation of the saints."

Much of my life has seemingly been wasted by sickness; still, the years I had fondly hoped to have spent in active service in promoting the latter-day work have not, I trust, been altogether unfruitful. I have had opportunities at home to testify to those who have visited me of the sustaining power of God. One thing I have learned, and prize more than gold or silver, is contentment with my lot. I have never known a time in my life when I could waste a moment in hopeless sorrow. . . .

It has been a hard struggle to give back to the Father the sweet spirits of children who for a time were so precious to me; but my greatest consolation is in knowing that my treasures are laid up in heaven safe from the contamination of sin. I have the satisfaction of knowing that the coming of the Savior is near, when those who sleep in the dust of the earth will arise and, with the faithful on earth, enter into the joys prepared for them before the foundation of the world.

Meanwhile, although our home is childless, our grand-children often fill the vacant places, and their tender love and childish prattle fill the void in our hearts, which for a long time we thought nothing could supply.

The memory of the famine and other privations through which I have passed serve to enhance the happiness of the years of comfort and plenty I have since enjoyed, and which still crown my path. . . .

In conclusion, I would say it is now twenty-nine years since, in my native land, I heard and obeyed the gospel as restored by an angel to Joseph Smith, the prophet of this dispensation, and gathered to this land that I might hear a living prophet make known the will of God to his people. And have I been disappointed? No, a thousand times, no. Though Joseph was slain, and Brigham Young, his successor, has gone behind the veil, a living prophet still leads and guides the Latter-day Saints.

Autobiography and Poems, pp. 62-64.

SISTER CROFT

"You Must Have Had a Wonderful Mother"

In the early days of the Southern States Mission, men of heroic mold were required to face persecutions and persist in their endeavors to reach the honest in heart. Many instances of heroism could be chronicled, but one of the most interesting was when a mother's letter played a very important part in saving a young elder from being cruelly whipped and possibly from being killed.

Elder Frank Croft was a missionary in the state of Alabama. Because he persisted in his legal rights guaranteed under the Constitution of the United States in preaching righteousness to the people, he was forcefully taken into a secluded spot of the backwoods for the purpose of receiving lashings across his bare back at the hands of armed and vicious men. Having arrived at the place where they had concluded to administer the torture, Elder Croft was commanded to remove his coat, shirt, and garments, and bare his body to his waist. Then he was stood against a nearby tree to which his arms and body were tied to prevent his moving while being lashed across the back until the blood would flow.

Having no alternative, he complied with the demands of the mob, but in so doing, there fell from his pocket a letter he had recently received from his mother who lived near Morgan,

Utah. Elder Croft, a short time before, had written his parents and in this letter had seriously condemned mob violence, the Ku Klux Klan, and others for their cowardly treatment of the elders. The letter that had fallen from his coat was an answer from his mother. In it she counseled, "My beloved son, you must remember the words of the Savior when He said, 'Blessed are they which are persecuted for righteousness' sake: for theirs is the kingdom of heaven'; also 'Blessed are ye, when men shall revile you and persecute you, and shall say all manner of evil against you falsely, for my name's sake. Rejoice, and be exceeding glad: for great is your reward in heaven: for so persecuted they the prophets which were before you.' Also remember the Savior upon the cross suffering for the sins of the world when he uttered these immortal words: 'Father, forgive them; for they know not what they do.' Surely, my boy, they who are mistreating you elders know not what they do, or they would not do it. Sometime, somewhere, they will understand and then they will regret their action and they will honor you for the glorious work you are doing. So be patient, my son; love those who mistreat you and say all manner of evil against you, and the Lord will bless you and magnify you in their eyes and your mission will be gloriously successful. Remember also, my son, that day and night, your mother is praying for you always."

Elder Croft, tied to the tree, was so situated that he could see that the leader of the mob had picked up the fallen letter and evidently had decided to read it before giving the word to his men to start the lashing. The elder observed the hardness of his features, the cruelty in his eyes. He then realized that no sympathy could be expected from him, for his every action was characteristic of cruelty and vindictiveness. He closed his eyes in resignation to his fate and, while awaiting the moment when the beating would begin, he thought of home and loved ones and particularly of his beloved mother. Then he silently uttered a prayer in her behalf.

Opening his eyes a moment or two later, and feeling that the leader had had time to finish reading the letter, he was amazed to see that the man had retired to a nearby tree stump and, having seated himself, was apparently reading the letter; but what was more amazing to the elder was the change in the man's countenance. Much of the hardness and cruelty in his face was gone; his eyes were slightly dimmed by moisture. His whole personality appeared to have changed. He would read a line or two or a paragraph and sit and ponder, and deep down in the elder's conscience was the hope—yes, the conviction—that the man's heart had been touched by the loveliness and beauty of his mother's letter.

To Elder Croft, it seemed that an interminable time had elapsed before the mob leader arose and, approaching the helpless elder, said: "Feller, you must have a wonderful mother. You see, I once had one, too." Then, addressing the other members of the mob, he said, "Men, after reading this Mormon's mother's letter, I just can't go ahead with the job. Maybe we had better let him go." Elder Croft was released and went his way, and the loving influence of his mother seemed very near.

Bryant S. Hinckley, *The Faith of Our Pioneer Fathers* (Deseret Book Co., 1956), pp. 257-59.

MARY L. CUTLER *

"Go to Zion"

"She shall not go with that deluded band of outlaws even though she has joined them." John Whitmore's face was white with fear and anger. "Send her to me immediately, and we shall see what she has to say for herself." His wife left the room, weeping softly to herself.

Mary, a beautiful twin girl of eighteen years, was singing merrily as she packed a small trunk with her most treasured belongings. "Your father wishes to see you at once." Mary's face sobered as she saw her mother's tears. She kissed her cheek and with an affectionate pat she left her. As she entered the living room, her father was pacing the floor nervously. A long talk between father and daughter followed in which Mary promised him if he would listen to the Mormon doctrine as she heard it, and if he did not believe in it, she would remain at home a year. The father was well pleased with this arrangement, for he was a Bible student and expected to corner the Mormons on their teachings.

The elder arrived and for three days and nights a hot discussion ensued. When it was finished, John Whitmore put his

---

°At eighteen years of age, and as a new convert to the Church, Mary L. Cutler left her family to cross the plains to her new home. She was a devoted wife and mother and also an accomplished singer. She died July 20, 1923, in Mesa, Arizona.

arm around his girl, gave her a father's blessing, and said, "Go to Zion! Mary, do the best you can. We may never live to get there."

It was a sad parting when Mary left father, mother, her twin sister Martha, and her other sisters, brothers, and friends. She never saw any of them again.

Roberta Flake Clayton, comp., *Pioneer Women of Arizona* (Mesa, Arizona, 1969), pp. 91-98.

ANNA STODDARD
MERRILL DAINES*

"Missionaries of Good Will"

I graduated from Utah Agricultural College in 1931, the same year that my husband, Robert Henry Daines II, whom I married on April 22, 1931, received his master's degree from the same college. He received a fellowship in plant pathology for the doctoral program at Rutgers University, so we moved to New Jersey at that time. These were Depression years, but we felt fortunate and blessed to have this opportunity.

Our plans, of course, were to return west as soon as Henry received his advanced degree. However, I suppose the Lord had other plans for us. When Henry received his Ph.D. in 1934 he was one of two of the doctoral graduates from the College of Agriculture at Rutgers University who received job opportunities. He was offered a position on the faculty of Rutgers, and this we gratefully accepted. Our main disappointment was that the Church was not strong in this area. It was not easy for our children to be raised in a non-Mormon community where they were the only Mormons in their schools and when prejudice against the Church was so strong.

*Sister Daines and her husband are the parents of two sons and two daughters. Brother Daines is president of the East Brunswick New Jersey Stake, and his wife is active in the stake Relief Society.

In 1944 we purchased our home in Metuchen. The first converts to the Church after our branch was organized were Brother and Sister Messeroll. They had been literally run out of Metuchen by their neighbors, ministers, and other townspeople after they had joined the Church. They expressed great fear about our being able to live in the home we had purchased.

One advantage we felt when we moved to Metuchen was the fine YMCA program there. We had always thought of the YMCA as being a good Christian institution with programs for our children that the Church at that time in our area could not provide. When we needed a place to meet locally in church, my husband went to the director of the Metuchen YMCA to see if we could rent their building for Sunday services, since they did not use their building on Sunday. The director said he thought it would be fine and most appropriate but that he would have to get permission from the board of directors, which met once a month.

We held church services in our home during this period and waited for a reply. After two months my husband went back to see if our request had been granted. The director was embarrassed to say that the board was having some trouble coming to a decision. A month or so later he called to say that our request had been turned down. This was a true Christian man, and he was so humiliated and distressed by the board of directors' action that he resigned his position in protest.

For many hours, my husband and I discussed how we could best solve this problem, and we prayed for guidance. We decided to enroll our oldest son in the YMCA program, and he and my husband took out a membership. There was a woman's auxiliary unit of the "Y" that raised funds for their youth programs and activities, so I joined that organization.

I offered my services every way I could, and by the second year I was elected president. I served two years in that capacity, then was elected a member of the board of directors. (Since this YMCA had a girls' program, there were women on the board as well as men.) Each term was for three years and, by the rules, each board member could serve only two terms. During these six years I worked diligently in every capacity I could and my husband did as much volunteer service as he had time for. Our second son joined when he was old enough, and both of our boys were active participants in the athletic programs.

After my first year of service as a member of the board of directors, a gentleman who was completing his second term as a director came to apologize to me. He said he had spearheaded the group of five people on the board who had rejected the Church request to rent the YMCA building for services. He said he had never known a Mormon before but had heard so many negative things about them that he had been attempting to keep Metuchen free from their influence. Then he expressed admiration for our family and the service we were rendering.

We tried to be an influence for good in other ways, one of which was through participation in PTA activities, where both my husband and I served as presidents. My husband also served two terms on the Metuchen board of education. When he was a candidate for his first term, there was an active "whispering campaign against the Mormons," so we were pleased when he polled the greatest number of votes of any of the candidates.

I feel that my husband and I and our children have tried to be missionaries of good will and understanding for the Church for these past forty-three years. I do not know of any ill will that now exists here against the Church or its programs.

MARGARET MILLER
DeWITT*

"I Was Dressed in My Wedding Finery"

When I was about twelve years of age, my sister Jane, six years older than I, joined the Mormon Church and immigrated to America a year or so later. The other members of the family felt that by so doing she had brought great disgrace to our family.

My mother died when I was twelve years old, and I lived with an older sister, Belle, who sold our home and rented one little room for the two of us. During this time my sister Jane wrote to me in care of a friend, Agnes McKay, urging me to attend the Mormon meetings and investigate their religion for myself. I did so secretly, going to their meetings when my sister supposed I was attending night school.

I was able to attend several meetings conducted by Mormon elders before my sister discovered my deception, which she finally learned from the girls at the factory where I worked. Thinking she was doing the proper thing, she gave me a severe whipping and warned me not to go near the elders again. However, this only served to strengthen my determination to find out for myself all about the Mormons and Mormonism.

---

*Margaret Miller DeWitt was born January 10, 1841, in Glasgow, Scotland. After she joined the Church and immigrated to America, she married Abel Alexander DeWitt. They were the parents of six children. Sister DeWitt died February 18, 1930.

I still continued my secret correspondence with my sister Jane, who lived in Holyoke, Massachusetts, and she sent me money to pay my passage across the ocean. I remember going to the bank and getting the money, which I concealed inside my dress in the daytime and in my shoe at night. Soon after this I left Belle's home. We had eaten breakfast, and I left as if I were on my way to the factory. I saw the clothes spread on the green to bleach (she had washed the day before) and I picked up my night cap and slipped it into my pocket. This was all I took with me except the clothes I had on.

I went directly to my friends, the McKays, who informed me that the next sailboat would not leave for two weeks. I couldn't go back home to Belle, so my kind Mormon friends, the McKays, hid me for two weeks in the home of a widow who boarded me. The McKays outfitted me with clothes for my journey.

Bills had been posted and rewards offered for my capture, so, fearing detection, I disguised myself when I went to the sailboat. Just before boarding the ship I posted a letter to my sister Belle telling her not to continue her search for me, as I was on my way to America. I crossed the gangplank and entered the ship. Then I went below into the steerage until the ship had started.

I then went up on the deck and took a last fond farewell of my native land. I was overcome with conflicting emotions as I saw it disappearing from my sight. For, though I was glad and eager to come to America where I could learn more about Mormonism and join my sister Jane, yet I felt sad to leave forever my native land and my brothers and sisters and friends. I extended my arms and cried, "Goodbye forever, old home," and the ship bore me off.

Soon after leaving I became violently seasick and lay on the bare deck for relief. Having taken nothing with me except my clothing, I had nothing to lie on. A young woman came near me, saying, "How's this? Haven't you folks to look after you? But no, I mustn't talk; I must do something."

She went to the cook room and made a little tea and toast. As I partook of it, my stomach became settled, so that I could get up and around. Soon I became adjusted to life on board ship. From Liverpool to New York, we were on the sailing vessel six weeks and three days.

When we landed at New York, Sister McKay's folks met us there. A large crowd was present as we were getting off the ship. I kept saying aloud, "Oh, have you seen my sister?" I hadn't heard the popular song being sung, entitled, "Oh, Have You Seen My Sister?" At once someone in that great throng caught up the words and sang it while the whole merry crowd began singing and laughing.

I took the train from New York to Springfield, Massachusetts, where my sister met me. Words cannot express the joy of our meeting. I went with her to her home in Holyoke. There I remained with her and a group of immigrant girls. We worked in a factory while earning the money to pay our way to Utah.

We worked in this factory for about three years. Our boardinghouse was managed by two old maid sisters who had rented a large house especially for factory girls. We paid them each month; outside of our board, lodging, and clothes, we saved *every cent* for our journey across the plains.

My sister left for Utah three weeks before I did, as there was not room for both of us in the first company. I handed to the president of the branch sixty dollars in cash to pay my way to Utah.

Before leaving for Zion, however, I had been baptized and confirmed a member of the Church. My sister and I had attended regularly the LDS services in Holyoke. Each meeting strengthened my faith, though I had believed the gospel to be true from the first time I heard the elders preach it in Glasgow. On account of the bitter opposition manifest by the anti-Mormons in Massachusetts, my baptism was performed at night. When I was taken to the river the ice was broken, and there I was baptized.

I traveled across the plains with Thomas Lyons and his invalid wife and five children. We were three months crossing the plains, under the captaincy of Edward Stevenson. My sister heard of the company through the Pony Express and was ready to meet me. She had arranged for a place for me to work—for a Sister Howard, who lived eight miles south of Salt Lake City at Big Cottonwood. My sister had a place in Salt Lake City and we often visited.

With the first money I earned in Salt Lake City I purchased a new chest for my clothes. It was made by Brother Thomas Ellerbeck, an excellent carpenter. I still have this chest and it is as good as new.

The date of our arrival was September 16, 1859, with 350 souls and 150 wagons. That evening in the Howard home, as I stood by the sink washing dishes, I noticed a young man come into the room—a tall, straight, handsome fellow. I nudged Sister Howard's daughter, who was wiping dishes, and asked, "Who is that?"

"Don't you get your heart set on him, because I already have my cap set for him," she answered. I replied that I did not want to fall in love with anyone. About six months later, however, when I was nineteen years old, this same young man became my husband. I had no parents to go to for advice, so when he proposed marriage, I went to Bishop Brinton and asked him to advise me. His answer was, "You'll make no mistake, Margaret, if you marry Aleck DeWitt."

Sister Howard had been like a mother to me; at the time of my marriage she dressed me completely in the very best of clothes. My wedding dress was a beautiful white, tucked all around the full skirt and trimmed with lace and white ribbon. Sister Howard engaged Eliza R. Snow and Sister Woodmansee to come to her home for a week and sew on my wedding dress, sheets, pillowcases, quilts, and everything preparatory for my marriage. I felt like a princess to be so honored.

The bishop who was to marry us was working on the jury that day, but he walked eight miles to our ward in order to perform the ceremony that night.

I had been afflicted with a sick headache during the afternoon and Sister Howard had sent me to bed. While I was there she and her daughters had fixed up the little two-room cottage that Brother DeWitt had rented for our future home. I was dressed in my wedding finery as we walked to the bishop's home, where we were married. Then we went to our little home.

I noticed that it was all lighted up; and when we entered, we beheld a table laden with a roasted chicken and everything that goes with it. My bed was all made up with new sheets and pillowcases and the beautiful quilt that Eliza R. Snow and Sister Woodmansee had made. We then spent a happy evening with the Howard family and the bishop's family. Mrs. Howard was an excellent cook, and the banquet she and her girls had prepared was delicious.

Brother DeWitt had brought a load of furniture from Salt Lake City; it had been unpacked and put in place. The new dishes were in a cupboard he had made. All this was a surprise to me.

Roberta Flake Clayton, comp., *Pioneer Women of Arizona* (Mesa, Arizona, 1969), pp. 105-109.

ALVERETTA S. ENGAR

"Longing to See My Mother"

It was a special Mother's Day program. A little mother gave the following testimony with a decidedly foreign, though highly pleasing, accent:

"About 25 years ago, in Dresden, Germany, when I was just a young girl, I was very ill; the missionaries were around me praying that I might get well. The final word came that in order to get better, a change of climate was necessary, and then I realized the full extent of a mother's love, for a few months later my dear mother began packing up things for her only daughter to be sent seven thousand miles away, perhaps never to see her again.

"The day finally came, with the promise to return in ten years. My mother had pretty brown hair; but the day I left I noticed that there were streaks of gray, which made me realize what she must have gone through to let her only daughter go. I came out here, was happily married in the temple, and was always planning when I could return to her. At times I would get quite homesick, so we would go up to a hill overlooking this beautiful valley and would dream of the time when I could go back; and oh! what a happy reunion it would be. But, sorry to say, ten years later, when I was going to return, sadness came into my life. My dear companion was taken, and I had three little children to take care of.

"On the day I was married I met a missionary who was also going to be married. We had become life-long friends, and instead of returning myself to see my mother, I saw this couple going on a pleasure trip to Germany.

"I had sent a letter telling Mama when they would start and on which steamer they would go; I also told her that they were tall, thin, dark people like the majority of Americans. My mother has a little flower store; there she sells the most beautiful roses, which she gets from Italy the whole year round. When this couple opened her door, she knew them, for she named them by their names! And with tears in her eyes my dear mother welcomed them as she would have done her own daughter.

"I shall never forget the day when this couple came back. It was in the evening and I had just put my little children to bed. While the travelers were telling me of their wonderful trip, it seemed as if I was living my childhood days all over again. And now I am going to tell you something, my brethren and sisters. As I sat there listening, the tears—no, they were not tears, it was water—were streaming down my face, for the longing to see my mother was so great.

"All the hopes have been given up of my ever returning to see her, but the Lord works in mysterious ways his wonders to perform, for the visit which I should have made years ago, I am in hopes will be made by my son when he is called on his mission to my homeland, and our daily prayers are that the dear mother, who tearfully said goodbye to her only daughter, may be kept well and strong to shower her mother-love upon her grandson."

Relief Society Magazine, May 1929, pp. 265-67.

AMY W. EVANS

"The Pioneer Woman"

As the Saints started across Iowa, it was decided to make stopping places where those who were not fully equipped with the necessary wagons, cattle, seeds, and provisions might have time to accumulate them. . . .

When it was found that these stopping places would be occupied for some time as the Saints started west, schools were established and land fenced, crops planted, and houses built. The women kept alive the spirit of home and the niceties of life. Social standards were not forgotten. At Mt. Pisgah, Lorenzo Snow's wife draped the walls of her rude log cabin with white sheets (carefully preserved); hollowed out turnips, which she tacked to the walls and used as candle holders; sprinkled fresh straw upon the dirt floor; and received her guests with dignity. After an evening of refined entertainment, she served refreshments consisting of succotash.

At this time a young couple and their children stopped to get together more supplies. The husband planted a garden and hurried to build a log cabin, for they were expecting another child very soon. He became ill but would not give up until the roof was on his house. Even then he went out to plant more seed, for they were determined to start the journey west next spring. He fell in the field and was carried to his cabin, terribly ill with fever. His young wife got up from her bed with her newborn child and watched him die. Her children were ill too, except five-year-old Susan. The widow begged that her husband be buried in a coffin, though many dead persons were being wrapped in blankets. Kind neighbors secured a wagon box from which a rude coffin was made, and little Susan went to her father's grave, the only one of the family able to do so. . . .

In the same company there was a cultured gentleman who was too weak to walk, so his beautiful young wife gave up the wagon to him, walking by its side, comforting and caring for him as best she could. When a buffalo was killed, she would exchange her share of the meat for a few crackers, a little fruit, or some dainty that her sick husband could eat. . . .

Sometimes circumstances demanded a sternness of woman foreign to her nature. This was the case with an English widow who, with her two sons, ages fourteen and sixteen, was making her way across the plains in the handcart company. One day her eldest boy lay down by their cart and said that he could not go farther. It was common at this stage of the journey for someone weakened from lack of food and worn out by toil to give up and die.

A group gathered around, and the mother came up. There lay her son, her main reliance; and he had given up. In this crisis, she sensed that extreme measures must be used. "Get up," she commanded. "I did not bring you here to die on the plains; you are going to Zion." Then she gave him a stinging slap in the face.

He was sixteen, and to be slapped by his mother in public made his blood boil. He needed no other stimulant. He jumped to his feet and pushed the cart along vigorously. For three days his anger kept him going.

As a white-haired man many years later, he maintained that this stern act of his mother saved his life. If she had weakened, he never could have gone on. They slept on the frozen ground, waded through the snow, and nearly starved before they reached their destination; but his mother's spirit and courage never wavered.

While the women on the plains carried with them the spirit of home, they also carried what they could of the culture of the race. In a barrel of beans or a bag of wheat—in fact, in any available place—they tucked away precious books, bits of rare china, pieces of real lace, some fine clothes, so that in the far-away new home things of beauty and culture should not be forgotten. . . .

At the World's Fair at San Francisco, there was a statue in honor of the pioneer woman, and on the pedestal was the following inscription: "Over rude paths beset with hunger and risk, she pressed on toward the vision of a better country; to an assemblage of men busied with the perishable rewards of the day she brought the threefold leaven of enduring society—faith, gentleness, and home, with the nurture of children."

<hr>

Relief Society Magazine, June 1930, pp. 329-31.

ANTONIA FLORES*

"He Took the Weight Out of My Hands"

Eleven years ago I was introduced to the gospel and was converted to The Church of Jesus Christ of Latter-day Saints.

One time several years ago, the branch president interviewed me to call me as Relief Society president. I was very afraid to be Relief Society president. I just didn't see how I could handle such a job and was afraid to tell him yes. Later that day, I remembered the principle of fasting and prayer. I fasted and prayed about accepting this position that I was so afraid of.

In the night, I had a revelation. I dreamed that I was walking, carrying a great weight in my hands. I had been walking a long time and was tired from carrying such a heavy weight. Then I saw our Lord Jesus Christ, and he took the weight out of my hands and invited me, saying, "Come, follow me." The next morning I felt wonderful; the fear had left me: I hurried to the branch president to tell what had happened, that I was no longer afraid and was sure it was right, and so, I have been able to continue working in the Relief Society several years as president with two wonderful counselors.

I have also had another great experience. I work as a

*Sister Flores is Relief Society president in the Tacna Branch of the Peru Lima Mission.

seamstress, and every time someone pays me for my work, I set aside one-tenth as my tithing. One time there was no money in the house; I didn't have even one cent other than the money I had set aside for tithing. It was Sunday, and time to pay my tithing at church.

My son, who was very small at the time, said to me, "But, Mama, if you pay your tithing today, what are we going to eat tomorrow?" I told him to have confidence in the Lord and He wouldn't let us go without food. So I went to church, paid my tithing, and came home with peace of mind, but still not knowing what we would do for our next meal, for we had absolutely no money. However, very early the next morning, a lady knocked on my door, bringing me material to make her a dress and paying me in advance for the work, and so we had money to live on the next day.

KATHRYN E. FRANKS

"A Valentine for Mother"

I must have been nine or ten, and I remember a February storm had just left the world outside snowy white. On the trees and fences the snow had drifted in unusual designs. In my own small bedroom the radiator hissed out in jerky sputters.

I was hiding in my bedroom, working on a fancy valentine for my mother. I had heavy red paper, real lace, white paper doilies, red ribbon, and a wonderful idea for Mother's valentine. I was the eldest, and it was important to me that mine would be the prettiest one my mother would receive.

The red heart was cut and the white lace nearly around the edge when my little sister Sara, who was four, came skipping into my room. She was trying to cut valentines from a make-it-yourself book.

"Oooh," Sara exclaimed when she saw what I was doing. "That is going to be beautiful! May I have some of your lace? I'm making a valentine for Mother too."

"No," I answered. "I'm busy. Don't bother me."

Sara looked disappointed. She stepped back. Without saying anything, she left the room.

After all, I remember thinking, if I give her all my ideas, her valentine will be as nice as mine.

Another few inches of lace were pasted around the heart when my younger brother Billy came bursting into my room. He had come home from school. "Look, sis," he said eagerly, "we're making these valentine nut cups for our mothers. I goofed. Mine are all messed up. Will you help me fix them?"

I knew then that if they were finished correctly they would be darling. They would make my valentine look pretty simple! "No," I scolded, tossing the cups at him. "I'm not going to have time to finish my own."

"All right," Billy said. "I'll take some of this lace and fix them myself."

I snatched away the lace and pushed him from the room. I was surprised when I saw Mother nearby, putting away clothes in the hall closet. I was sure she hadn't seen what I was working on, but I was certain she had overheard all the nasty things I'd said. Her face looked sad.

At bedtime I carefully placed all the trimmings with the partly made valentine in a big box, ready for school the next day. Miss Rodgers, our teacher, had promised us that we could work on our valentines the next afternoon during our art period.

I remember how excited I was when it was time to clear our desks and start to work. I wanted to finish the outside of mine, so I could start thinking of a special verse. It had to be ready for the next morning, Valentine's Day.

As Miss Rodgers handed out the red paper and the trimmings, the children crowded around my desk. "Look!" they exclaimed. "It's going to look just like a store valentine." Miss Rodgers stopped to admire it. She complimented me on my idea.

I was certain then—this was going to be the nicest valentine my mother had ever received.

The children were asked to take their seats quickly. Miss Rodgers stood in front of the class and began her instructions on how to make valentines. First, we were to fold the red sheet and cut the heart.

"You know," she told us, "it doesn't matter how you plan your design, or if there is any design on the front at all. It's the message inside that counts. The words 'I love you' are what really matter. Your mother knows by your actions how much you love her."

Miss Rodgers said other things about the real meaning of Valentine's Day, but I couldn't watch her any longer, or listen to what she was saying. I think I gazed down a long time at my valentine. I fingered it lightly. I was looking at the valentine, but as a child, I was seeing myself quite clearly. I'd forgotten, I guess, what I was going to write inside. My valentine didn't look pretty to me anymore. I placed it back in the box and decided to work on it after school. I was no longer in the mood. There were some things I wanted to do before I finished my mother's valentine.

I hurried home after school. I found Sara and asked her into my room. There I took her wrinkled book and showed her how to cut the hearts out straight. I tried to be patient while her small hands cut crookedly.

Mother knocked on my door to inform me my friend had come to play. I told her I'd be out later, after I had finished helping Sara.

When Billy came home I sent him to wash his hands so we could work on his nut cups. I showed him how to paste the small red paper hearts on the outside and trim the tops with lace. "As soon as we finish," I told Billy, "we'll take our allowance and you can ride your bike to the store for some tiny red hearts and some assorted nuts. We'll fill them and have the cups ready for tomorrow."

Billy was delighted with the idea. It felt good to be the eldest. "They look swell, sis. Thanks for helping me." Then he scooted out of the room with the money to go to the store.

That evening I put Sara to bed and read her a story. I dried the dishes before going to my room to begin my schoolwork. First, I tried to think of a good verse for Mother's valentine, but I was too sleepy. I couldn't think. I remember how confidently I put it aside until the next morning. I turned out the lights and slipped under the covers.

I overslept the next morning. When I woke up I heard Billy and Sara in the hallway already giving Mother their valentines.

I can feel it now, how near the tears were. Hastily I pulled out the fancy, unfinished valentine from the box. I scrambled for the paste and lace—a verse. There wasn't time. I had to dress or I'd miss the school bus. All I could do was open the valentine and write in my handwriting, "I love you, Mother," and sign my name.

Funny thing about mothers. There was a proud smile on her face when I handed it to her, like a secret message between us. I think she loved that valentine more than any I ever made, or any I ever bought her afterwards.

How am I sure? Perhaps I wasn't, not until I became a mother and today I received my first such valentine!

Relief Society Magazine, February 1966, pp. 107-109.

Biographical Sketch

RUTH HARDY FUNK

Ruth Hardy Funk was born in Chicago, Illinois, a daughter of Dr. T. Fred and Polly Reynolds Hardy. A graduate of the University of Utah, she was married to Dr. Marcus C. Funk December 31, 1938, in the Salt Lake Temple; they have four children and five grandchildren.

Sister Funk has been active in civic affairs and professional organizations and taught choral music at East High School in Salt Lake City. She has served on the general board of the Young Women's Mutual Improvement Association and as a member of the Adult and Youth Correlation committees of the Church. In November 1972 she was called to serve as young women's general president of the Aaronic Priesthood MIA, now known as the Young Women of the Church.

RUTH HARDY FUNK

"No, President Lee, We Accept"

I had not been a professional teacher, but the tragic death of Miss Lorraine Bowman, music director at East High School, just before school began, caused me to step in and open the door for the young music students.

It was during my fourth year of teaching that the telephone rang at noon one day in the office adjoining the a cappella choir rehearsal room. It was my husband, Mark. He told me to sit down.

I wasn't used to his calling me, because I was usually in classes all day, so I was sure that something was wrong with one of the children. However, he assured me that they were all right—but I really must sit down. I did. Then he said that Arthur Haycock, secretary to President Harold B. Lee, had just called and asked if he would bring me with him to see President Lee at four o'clock.

Mark relates my reaction this way: "Have you ever been on the other end of a telephone while someone cries for fifteen minutes and you can't say a word?" That's exactly what happened. Although I didn't know why I had been called to see President Lee, just the anticipation of being in the Prophet's presence was very humbling.

We kept the appointment and were with President Lee for

one hour. He spoke of the youth and of his love and concern for them; his absolute confidence in them; the need for every possible way and means of love and leadership to be extended to them, for they truly were a choice generation, and they were being prepared for very special problems and leadership.

After a long discussion, President Lee turned directly to my husband and said, "Brother Funk, we would like your permission to ask your wife to be the president of the Aaronic Priesthood MIA for Young Women."

Then these two great servants of the Lord—President Lee and my husband—had a rather lengthy conversation, it seemed to me, as I sat listening. They talked about how I love youth, how I love those with whom I work every day, about our grand family, about many intimate and beautiful things. Then President Lee said, "Brother Funk, would you like to fast and pray about it and then let me know?" At that point my husband turned to me—he could just barely reach my hand—and said, "No, President Lee, we accept."

This is the way one is called through the priesthood of God—through one's husband. Oh, girls, what beautiful experiences you have as you share this priesthood with your husbands!

Address to the student body of Ricks College, Rexburg, Idaho, October 30, 1973.

→←

RUTH HARDY FUNK

"You're Ready, My Dear"

Last year, standing in the wings behind the curtain moments before a magnificently inspiring young artists' music festival, I witnessed a performance that touched my heart—maybe even more than the performance on the stage, but certainly as much.

A prayer had been offered in behalf of each of the young performers that their hard weeks—yes, even years—of conscientious preparation might be drawn from at this moment to ensure a masterful performance. Eyes were moist; hearts were touched as strength and unity of family members lent confidence and encouragement to each performer. At that moment a father, appearing proud and grateful, quickly leaned forward, gave his beautiful young daughter a tender kiss on the cheek, and whispered, "You're ready, my dear." And her next step was on stage, alone—a solo flight.

Oh, that our preparation at each step in our lives might be such that, as we approach that hour of challenge (and there are many), we might have that quiet whispering of the Spirit in our ears: "You're ready, my dear." Readiness implies so much and demands much more. Just a few of the requirements are discipline, teachableness, understanding, humility, faith, and practice.

Each one of us has a specific destiny, which God intends we shall receive according to our faithfulness. He has a place for each of us and prepares us each day to receive it if we are worthy. Everything in our lives is there for a purpose, and that purpose is to prepare us. Preparation precedeth all readiness. Are we ready to receive the sacrament, the companionship of the Holy Ghost, a comprehension of the Lord's atoning sacrifice? Our Father in heaven is anxious to open the windows of heaven to us just as soon as we are prepared and ready.

"Ready to Receive," BYU devotional assembly, May 1974.

"What Does the LDS Church Offer Its Young Women?"

We affirm that women have many roles and many options, but that their central role, from which all others radiate as the spokes of a wheel, is the role of wife and mother. To those who ask, "But what if a woman chooses not to accept that role? What if she doesn't want it?" I must say, in all directness and honesty: a woman who has chosen to love God and serve him by keeping all his commandments *does* want that role. The two options go together naturally.

The love of God engenders confidence that his commandments are not arbitrary but logical, that they form a woman's map for reaching her maximum joy and fulfillment. It is not that she must choose this option if she loves the Lord; it is rather that she wants to. Not marriage and motherhood at any cost, of course, and certainly not marriage and motherhood or forfeiting her dignity and her status. If these roles cannot be achieved in righteousness in this life, they can be realized in eternal progression. To us, there is no higher fulfillment. The very highest title to which a man in our Church can aspire is the title of father, which is what our God himself uses most often as his own title. So it is with woman. The highest title to which she can aspire is mother.

Let me say to the women of the world everywhere: We as women of The Church of Jesus Christ of Latter-day Saints are with you in every wholesome pursuit. We too are dedicated to the fulfillment of women, and we know that historically women have been wronged, at various times and in various places. We began long ago to right these wrongs. As Belle S. Spafford, immediate past president of our Relief Society, the largest organization of women in the world, has said: "The liberation of all women began with the organization of this Church." But in righting these wrongs, let us not throw out the good with the bad, the eternal with the temporal. As you labor to improve the lot of women, we invite you to explore more thoroughly just exactly what it is that our church does offer young women, mature women—and men as well. We believe we can offer not only help in any cause that is righteous, but divine wisdom to distinguish the good from the evil. And we assure you of our comradeship and good will. After all, remember that we called each other "sister" long before it was fashionable!

What does the LDS Church offer its young women? It offers them a place to stand amid the chaos around them. It offers them the calm of the eye of the hurricane. It offers them eternal perspective and an identity from which to view the particular vistas of the last third of the twentieth century. It offers them inner peace without which no external progress can take on meaning.

Address at women's conference sponsored by the Women's Resource Center, University of Utah, October 1974.

EILEEN GIBBONS *

"Mother Is the Real Miracle"

"**M**other, it's for you!" Three daughters who used to dash for the telephone every time it rang and answer with an anticipant "Hi!" now calmly raise it from the hook, mutter a calm "Hello," and sigh, "Mother, it's for you."

Listen closely, and you can hear them add to themselves, "It's always for you!"

You see, I'm one of the three daughters, and my mother is the president of a ward Relief Society. She's relatively new in the job, but during the months she has been president, we girls, our four brothers, and our father have witnessed a miracle.

Miracles aren't exactly unusual in big families. Ours has managed to remain happy through periods of economic depression, broken teenage hearts, the cruel adolescent teasings of too many freckled-faced brothers, and the mischief of a seven-year-old named Ted.

But Mother is the real miracle. For as long as we can remember, she has been doing extra, unusual things to save time, effort, and money. Rising at 5 A.M. to pick raspberries on shares, midnight wall-papering parties, and the care of ten pens of rab-

---

*Eileen Gibbons Kump, a free-lance writer, is now a mother herself and helps her husband, Ferrell, in his Church assignments. They reside in St. Joseph, Missouri.

bits are among her "saving" ideas. Add to these washing, ironing, cleaning, and cooking for nine, and you have someone much too busy to sit and visit, read a good book, or call on a neighbor for a friendly chat. Yet, these are the things every busy housewife hopes someday to find time to do.

That's why when Mother told us the bishop wanted her to be president of the Relief Society we all gasped, "When?"

Mother already moved from one job to another like lightning and was the first awake and the last to bed. We'd chastised her plenty of times about moving too fast, and now the Church wanted to give her one of its biggest jobs. For several days we talked about it.

"She's just the person, but . . ."

"Wouldn't she be wonderful! But . . . ?" and then there was just the plain, "But, Mother!"

Of course Mother said yes. She had already said yes when we were going around the house wondering "When?" to ourselves and saying, "But . . ." to her.

At the time, Mother was in the Primary presidency and theology teacher in the Relief Society. She was baking twelve loaves of bread every week and was keeping a surplus of canned food in the basement and frozen food in the locker. She also spent an hour every day helping the child up the street improve his reading so he could be promoted. She was also giving several minutes a day to Larry because he needed tangible encouragement while he practiced the piano.

Torn denim knees had a way of appearing, and old rags had to be made into rugs. It was too expensive for the girls to buy all their clothes, and as long as shirts and trousers could be made from Dad's old suits and our too-small cottons, the little boys would wear them homemade.

A new latch on the door, new paint in the bedroom, the buckle torn from a shoe—a myriad of little jobs were already appearing daily and Mother was squeezing them in.

And now the bishop wanted her to . . .

We girls told her how happy we were, at the same time gesturing melodramatic stories about how we would probably have to quit school and our jobs so Mother could work in the Relief Society.

That was several months ago, and Mother is still busy because she still has seven children and the jobs that go along with a big family. Of course, we all have to help a little more, but the miracle is still there. Mother has been able to do the job, keep up her home, and bring a new spirituality, enthusiasm, and happiness into her relations with her family. This is the miracle. She has more time and energy than she has ever had before.

"Mother, it's for you" calls her to the phone at least a dozen times every day. Someone feels she ought to let Mother know that Sister Wallace is ill. Her first counselor phones to say, "Sure we can go visiting the shut-ins this afternoon!"

Perhaps it's a death in the ward. That usually means food to prepare, comfort to give, an assortment of needs to fill. There are flowers to arrange and children to tend.

Meetings need to be planned, work days scheduled, positions filled—the usual duties of a president. And Mother does them.

She has found time to do them well, along with her washing, sewing, cooking, cleaning, and the multitude of other household jobs that come unexpectedly.

If you tiptoe into her room almost any evening, you'll find her sitting up in bed reading a good book, the newspaper, or a magazine—to her a luxury. And it isn't late. Only the little boys are in bed. But you see, Mother is tired at night as always. She still has much to do, and we still tell her she does it too swiftly.

But she is a new woman. There is contentment instead of exhaustion after a day of hard work. There is joy at every chance to help, expressions of gratitude from the helped. There is love between her and a hundred women she never knew before. Most of all, there is a realization and a firm testimony in her heart that wards are living, complex units that need a mother.

And the children? We enjoy our miracle mother, and it hasn't hurt us girls at all to cook a little more often, sew on a few buttons ourselves, or even to think now and then that "he" surely would have called, if Mother hadn't been president of the Relief Society.

Relief Society Magazine, May 1954, pp. 298-99.

Biographical Sketch

ETHELYN GRAHAM

Ethelyn Graham, a member of the general committee of the Church's Young Women's organization, resides in Bountiful, Utah. She and her husband, Rodney Graham, division manager of Husky Oil Company, have three children, Sheri, Jeff, and Lisa.

Prior to her assignment with the Young Women, Sister Graham served on the Youth Correlation Committee of the Church. She has also had extensive experience in working with youth in the MIA as well as teaching in Sunday School and serving as a Relief Society president. She filled a Spanish American mission.

An active civic worker, Sister Graham has been a hospital volunteer, PTA president, and March of Dimes volunteer. At the time of her call to the Young Women's committee, she was assistant director of the Career Information Center at the University of Utah. Previously she had been employed in the university's placement center.

ETHELYN GRAHAM

"Perfect Vision"

Presiding Bishop Victor L. Brown placed his hands upon my head and in the first sentence of the blessing promised me perfect vision. The words that followed strengthened and lifted me. The warmth of his strong hands and those of my husband on my head gave me peace and reassurance. But emblazoned deep in every fiber of my being were the words "perfect vision." Through eyes that had been less and less perfect during the preceding months, I looked on this great man with gratitude and love as we shook hands and parted.

My husband and I made our way from his office and home to await our appointment with the specialist who would tell us what had to be done with my eyes. As the examinations dragged on through most of the afternoon, the words "perfect vision" went over and over in my mind—not "good," not "improved," but "perfect." In view of other things pronounced in that blessing, it didn't really surprise us too much to have the doctor return to the room where we were waiting to announce that he had acquired two perfect eyes, one of which he felt I should have.

Shortly before 9 P.M. I was taken to surgery. Introductions were made all around; this in itself was a bit unusual, but the operation was done with a local anesthetic and I was conscious throughout the entire time.

Through the two and one-half hours that followed, some conversation ensued and some questions were answered, but for the most part my talk was with my Father in heaven, whose presence was very close. The peace of mind and sense of joy at what he had in store for me occupied my thoughts part of the time, and I wondered what I might be able to learn from this experience and how better I might function in his kingdom when I had met and conquered this trial. Near midnight I was returned to my room, having partaken of a miracle—the cornea transplant was complete. All the events of that day came through to me in a hazy, half-reality. It was as though I had been witnessing it on a movie screen but had read the book before. Some of the details were new, but the story was totally familiar.

I had been privileged to know something of the events that were going to take place in my life. Some eight weeks prior to that eventful night I had sat in the office of Ardeth Kapp, second counselor in the Young Women's general presidency. (At the time I was a member of the general board and working under her direction.) So strong had been the holy promptings of the preceding days that I felt I had to tell her what I knew to be true. I told her that I knew the condition of my eyes was serious and that the news I was to hear from my doctor that day would not be good news. It was also clear to me that there would be many days when the news would not be good and there would be very difficult days through which I must pass. But far more important than that was the sense of joy and expectation for what the Lord had in store for me. The only parallel I could relate to was that I felt as though I had been given a difficult new call that both honored and frightened me. I had an abiding assurance that I was being watched over and protected. Sister Kapp's strength, love, and deep faith lifted and sustained me, and I knew why I had felt inclined to share my news.

The weeks passed, and after many hours in doctors' offices and various attempts to contain, if not correct, the condition, it became obvious that surgery was inevitable. My family had fasted and prayed for me, but now the members of my general board family invited us to join them for a special day of fast, which we concluded with an early morning temple session. During the special prayer that was offered in my behalf my heart was filled with thanksgiving, not only for the goodness of my Father in heaven to me, but also for the manifestation of the way the gospel of Jesus Christ makes literal brothers and sisters of us all.

It has now been almost nine months and there remains ahead the task of fitting a correction so that workable vision will be there. Much of the difficult path still lies ahead, and yet I can count many more blessings than problems associated with this experience. The thrill of seeing our children respond and grow with the demands made upon them has touched our hearts. Jeff, at twelve, did his homework beside me as I tried for the first time to use the automatic ironer, ready to release it in case I had problems. Eight-year-old Lisa helped prepare meals, read to me by the hour, and polished bathrooms with untiring enthusiasm. Sheri managed to come home each weekend from the hectic final semester life at BYU to cook, clean, wash, iron, and brighten our spirits. My husband found a myriad of happy ways to make me glad we're together for time and eternity.

The Relief Society sisters tape-recorded meetings, brought singing quartets to my home, and in general brought sisterhood to me. Tape recordings of the scriptures brought the words of the Savior to life for me, and I knew the sensation of having him talk to me personally. Chief among the joys during those days was release from any responsibilities outside my home and family. I almost felt guilty that I was enjoying so much just cooking (even though at times I had to use a magnifying glass to read recipes and spice labels), dusting, light cleaning, and caring for my family.

The joy of having time to feel and smell spring come to our valley was almost beyond description, despite the fact that I was seeing little of it. I spent the warm days in my yard, working in the flowerbeds, lying on the grass, having small parties with the children, and walking miles and miles through our town after I had conquered curbs and street crossings. It was during these days of new awakenings and realizations that another truth began to dawn upon me. Those beautiful words, "perfect vision," had come and gone through my thoughts a million ways, and now I was beginning to understand that perfect vision comes from within. In not seeing, I was learning to feel with different intensity and dimension than I had ever felt. The sounds and smells I had taken for granted were now so precious and exciting

I could not believe their beautiful impact. The nearness on a day-to-day basis of my Father in heaven was a touching reality. A new closeness to the Savior was emerging and my commitment to his work reached deep into me. Life had never been more beautiful or precious.

At this point the prospect lies ahead of going through a similar course with the other eye, and I find that same constant, sweet, peaceful spirit to draw from. I find a few of the same anxieties tugging at me, but for the most part I feel a quiet assurance that all has proceeded on schedule and will continue to do so. A valuable new knowledge is also mine—that, regardless of the outcome to physical vision, I have already been brought nearer to "perfect vision" than ever before, and for this I am eternally grateful.

(Note: Since this experience was written, Sister Graham has undergone her second transplant, which was so successful, she writes, that "I came right from surgery without needing medication for pain, without the slightest hurt. . . . The vision in the first transplant is improving daily, and my life is moving back into its former high gear.")

❯━━━❯

ETHELYN GRAHAM

"A Sacred Trust"

The sharp ring of the telephone cut through the quiet of our home one night at about 11:30. Somehow calls at unusual hours always bring fears and quickened heartbeats. When I reached the phone, I heard the voice of the father of one of the girls I had taught a few years before. "Sister Graham," he almost sobbed, "you are the only person Jan will talk to. You just have to help us."

Of course, I told him, I would be glad to help. Why, I had been working with and helping this girl for quite some time, and no one was more aware than I that she needed me. So why did I feel so sick inside as I listened to this good father pour out his heart and plead for my help? Why was I searching my soul so intently for the answer? Why was I less concerned for the immediate problem than for the far more alarming realization that was sweeping over me?

With a heartache that brought tears to my eyes I suddenly realized that I had been guilty of a very serious sin—I had unknowingly been leading a trusting young girl away from her father and mother. How could I have presumed that my love and caring could in any way balance that of a caring mother and father? I somehow forced a composure that allowed me to comfort the father and offer the help necessary. My silent prayers were mixed with pleas for forgiveness and a solemn resolve never again to draw a young person from the divine stewardship of caring mother and father.

That painful night passed. Indeed, for that one night and for a period shortly after, I was the only person who could help my young friend. But no one worked more anxiously than I in the coming weeks to build back the family bridges I had helped to erode by my solicitous "understanding." Leading her back to her parents who cared for her, despite some conflicts in the home, was fortunately far easier than I had imagined.

Painful though the experience was, I learned that one who sets his hand to do the Savior's work must know the core principles of his gospel well in order to keep proper balance and not betray his sacred trust.

———◆———

MARY GRAHAM

"Give All That You Have for the Gospel's Sake"

As told by Robert D. Young

When my mother, Mary Graham, was about fourteen years old, her father was lying on his deathbed. An elder of the Church came to the door with a tract, telling of the restoration of the gospel. Her father read the tract and said, "Mary, my girl, that is true. I believe that young man has come with the true gospel. Search out this true gospel and embrace it."

After the death of her father (her mother had died some years before), the orphaned Mary became a servant girl in the wealthy Allen family. When they learned she was investigating Mormonism, they angrily told her she was injuring their business by attending these meetings. People were beginning to think the Allens were sympathetic with this unpopular religion.

One dark and rainy night the Allen family assembled and called Mary before them. Bitterly the father said, "Mary, there is the door. You take your choice right now. Either our home and give up Mormonism, or out of our home into the night." She cried about it. Naturally she would like to stay, but she could not renounce the gospel, for she knew it was true. The homeless Mary walked out into the bleak night with only a shilling in her pocket. That shilling she paid to a friend of her father, who rented to her his hall in which the elders could preach.

111

Friends were raised up for Mary. She obtained other employment, married, and had a family of thirteen children, born in Scotland. In 1872 they came to Utah. When they arrived in Salt Lake City, the Allen family was there to welcome them and took them to their home for a wonderful banquet. "You are the cause of our being in the Church," they declared.

When Mary had so courageously left their home in Scotland rather than give up the true faith, the Allen family had concluded that her religion must be something extraordinary. They knew her as one of the sweetest, best, and most beautiful girls of their acquaintance. Mr. Allen had said, "I cannot help but feel that there is something more to Mormonism than we understand; it cannot be just a man-made religion." He and his family had investigated, joined the Church, emigrated to Utah, and then welcomed Mary and her family when they arrived.

Just before her death, Mary, my mother, called her children to her and told them this story and said, "You may never be asked to give all that you have for the gospel's sake, but if you are, give your all. I am eighty years of age, and I have never wanted. So I leave this with you my children, that even if it takes the last cent you have for the Church, give it gladly. It is the finest thing you can ever do."

At her death in 1911, she had 125 descendants. All of them have been inspired by her example and her testimony.

Improvement Era, January 1965, p. 33.

PHEBE ADAMS HANCOCK

"Don't Spend That Five Dollars"

Phebe Adams Hancock was well acquainted with the Prophet Joseph Smith. Alta O'Driscoll, her great-granddaughter, relates:

"She told me that when she was to give birth to her fifth child, she had saved the money from her eggs for eight months to buy the baby's clothes, and having five dollars and two dozen eggs she rode with her husband, Solomon, thirty miles on a board over a wagon bed, happy to be on the way to town for a day of shopping.

"When she arrived, she traded out her two dozen eggs, buying two yards of factory or unbleached muslin. She brought out the cherished five dollars to spend when Solomon touched her shoulders and said, 'Phebe, don't spend that five dollars. I am impressed that you must not spend it.'

"My great-grandmother, being just as human as you or I, left the store angry and her eyes filled with tears. She and Solomon had driven twenty miles toward home without speaking when Joseph Smith rode up out of a deep wash and said, 'Solomon, we are hungry.' My great-grandfather proudly handed him the five dollars. Joseph Smith waved the bill over his head and said to those with him, 'Brethren, I told you God would provide.'

"Great-grandmother told Solomon she was sorry and that she could manage with two yards of muslin, and she did."

Kate B. Carter, *comp.*, *Heart Throbs of the West* (Daughters of the Utah Pioneers), vol. 9, p. 30.

◄――――►

HELENA HANNONEN

"It Was Hard to Be Different"

In the early summer of 1960 two young men were pedaling their bicycles up and down the streets of Lappeenranta, Finland, knocking on doors and talking to people; we could tell that they were foreigners. To us children this was exciting, and we missed no opportunity to hear what the neighbors had to say about the Mormons.

Then one evening my widowed mother told my brother and me that she couldn't believe the unkind things that were being said about these missionaries, and she didn't like the way they were being treated. She said she was going to give them a chance to come to our home and tell their message. How grateful I am for her Christian spirit!

The elder who taught us spoke very little Finnish. Often he asked us children if we understood what he said, and we did. He explained the gospel simply and beautifully, and we were all baptized in August of that year.

At school for many years I was the only Latter-day Saint. Although it was hard to be different and accept the unkind comments and actions of my classmates, I often told myself, "Dare to be different!" Gradually I overcame the fear of being hurt by the unkindness of others. I didn't isolate myself, but learned to face people and respect their right to be different too.

When I was twelve, I had my first debate with my religion teacher. My answer to a question was influenced by the beliefs taught by The Church of Jesus Christ of Latter-day Saints, and the teacher said I was wrong. As I stood and listened to her, I could feel the Spirit of the Lord with me, and I was able to quote passages from the Bible to support my statements. Finally, she had no more answers. From that day I had a testimony that the Lord listens to our honest, humble pleading.

My mother, though physically weak, was spiritually strong; she helped me walk in the way I had chosen, leading with a firm but gentle hand. Instead of spending my evenings in the dark, smoky cafes that were popular among the youth, I was encouraged to study music, art, books, and sports. Soon I had the respect of my classmates and was a leader among them.

Every time my class at school was asked to conduct the morning religious service, they wanted me to present the views of my faith to the whole student body. My class supported me by replacing the singing of their church hymns with recordings of the Mormon Tabernacle Choir.

Seven years went by, and my religion teacher asked me to give a fifteen-minute presentation in class about the Church. The question-and-answer session that followed took the next two class periods. Then the teacher came to me and said she knew I was right, and she was ready to read the Book of Mormon.

I have been blessed with rich experiences, and the Savior has been my shepherd, my light, and my special friend during all the years of my youth.

Ensign, July 1974, p. 42.

IDA RACHEL HAYCOCK

"You May Burn It!"

The leader of the mob was a large, burly, and murderous demon. He told Grandmother if she would denounce Mormonism he would not set fire to her home. Her strength and faith in our gospel was very strong and she faced this wicked man with defiance and dignity, stomping her foot and saying, "You may burn it!" His answer was, "I'll give you twenty minutes to get out."

With the help of her seven children she gathered the most necessary and needful articles and threw them into a wagon. There was no time for packing. She had no team of horses, but she had one ox and a cow. The boys yoked them together to the wagon and drove away, bidding farewell to their home.

Grandmother suddenly remembered a fat pig ready to kill, so she sent the boys back to see if it had been spared. It was burned to a crisp. They joined a company of Saints who were on their way to Council Bluffs.

Kate B. Carter, comp., *Treasures of Pioneer History* (Daughters of the Utah Pioneers), vol. 3, p. 179.

◆━━◆

SISTER JOHNS

"One of Us Must Go Home"

It was one Sunday in the winter of 1906. We had just moved from our tiny mud-thatched log house into our partially completed new home. We were using some of the bedrooms and the dining room, while in some of the others, amid the shavings were stored the workbench and lumber for finishing the house.

It was nearly meeting time. Our eldest child, a boy, had gone to see his grandma. We were expecting him to return any minute so I cheerfully left our little girl in charge of our other children—a year-old baby, a little girl of five, and a boy of three—and went to meeting.

I enjoyed the services very much until it was time for the sacrament. Then a feeling came over me that I ought to go home. I did not wish to go—Brother Smith, a son of John Henry, was to speak to us that day.

We were holding services in the schoolhouse, and as the feeling that I should go home became stronger each moment, I put my elbows on the desk in front of me and put my head in my hands and prayed that the feeling might continue. There was no doubt now. The feeling—I know no word that better expresses it—became stronger than ever. My husband was sitting just across the aisle. I wrote him a note saying, "One of us must go home," and instantly left the room. My husband immediately came out and when I told him my feelings he said, "I'll go home." I was content then and went back into church, while he took the team and drove rapidly away.

What a sight met his eyes! Our eldest daughter was by the window, her back to the room, singing and rocking the baby while the little boy and girl were filling the kitchen range with shavings from the other room, leaving a path from the bench to the stove. Just as my husband opened the outer door some of the flaming shavings fell among those scattered on the floor. The fire was between the children and the outside door; soon the house would have been a mass of flames and the children imprisoned within its walls. I am indeed thankful that I received the warning, that my husband arrived in time to extinguish the flames, and that we were spared the horror of returning to a blazing home.

Juvenile Instructor, April 1914, p. 242.

KAAOAOLAHILAHI KAILIKINI

"She Understood"

As told by Roscoe C. Cox

Sister Kaaoaolahilahi Kailikini—translated, her name means "the thin side of Indian"—was perhaps as fine a specimen of true Hawaiian womanhood as I ever met in my early six and a half years among those wonderful people.

Tall, stately, heavy—weighing perhaps 250 pounds—she was kind, considerate, gentle, and generous, and had an undying faith in the gospel of Jesus Christ. When I met her, she was probably about sixty years old and was serving as president of the Relief Society in Kokoiki Branch, Kehala District, on the island of Hawaii.

She was one of the then quite numerous Hawaiians who had made no effort whatever to learn any language other than her own. She was entirely incapable of making an "r" or an "s" sound, letters not in the Hawaiian vocabulary. *"Iseu Kristo"* always came out *"Ieku Kaliko."*

It was on Tuesday, February 8, 1921, that we received word that a handsome young apostle, David O. McKay, and his traveling companion, Hugh J. Cannon, were in the islands and, accompanied by our mission president, E. Wesley Smith, would visit Hawaii. All missionaries on that island were instructed to gather at Hilo on February 11.

120

First there was a five- or six-hour missionary meeting, which no one wanted to see come to an end. Then came a luau and some of the best Hawaiian music to be had in the islands.

A well-attended public meeting was held in the Hilo Branch chapel in the evening. From the stand I saw Sister Kailikini in the audience and took special notice of her. Her face lighted up as President Smith made introductory remarks in Hawaiian, but she seemed puzzled as President Cannon spoke. Then her whole countenance beamed as Elder McKay spoke.

As soon as possible after the meeting I hurried to her and asked her how she had liked the meeting. "Oh, it was wonderful!" she exclaimed.

"Are you sure you are not fibbing a bit?" I asked. "It was all in English, and you could not understand it."

She put her hands on my shoulders and, looking me in the eye, with tears running down her cheeks, replied, "*O na hualolelo aole au i maopopo. Aka, of ka Uhane, oia ka'u i maopopo ai.*" ("The words I did not understand. But that spirit—that I understood.")

Then she told me briefly what Elder McKay had said, how on three occasions during the day clouds had briefly hidden the sunshine. He had said this reminded him of three shadows that had come to the Hawaiians: (1) some of the evils brought by the white man, (2) the Hawaiians had lost the land, and (3) they may have lost their land partly because of natural generosity, but also partly because of laziness. She said he urged young people present to acquire land, hold on to it, and reestablish the Hawaiian people as an independent, self-supporting race.

Sister Kailikini probably did not understand a single word the visiting apostle said, but she certainly got his message!

Improvement Era, September 1967, pp. 7-8.

Biographical Sketch

ARDETH G. KAPP

Ardeth G. Kapp was born in Cardston, Alberta, Canada, a daughter of Edwin Kent and June Leavitt Greene. She was graduated from Brigham Young High School in Provo, Utah, and received an associate degree from Weber State College, the bachelor of science degree in education from the University of Utah, and a master's degree in curriculum development from Brigham Young University.

She has taught in the Davis County schools in Utah and also in a series of television programs for the Utah Network for Instructional Television. For five years she was on the faculty of the College of Education at BYU.

In the Church, she served on the Youth Correlation Committee and is now second counselor in the Young Women's organization.

She and her husband, Heber G. Kapp, have dedicated their lives to strengthening the lives of youth, and young and old alike find welcome in their home.

ARDETH G. KAPP

"Would He Ever Call Again?"

The following is an account of a young girl who grew up in a small rural community with limited educational opportunities. The first day of her senior year she found herself without friends, entering the high school in what seemed to her to be a big city. Having lost her way and arriving late, her anxiety was only intensified after she quickly observed that she not only didn't know her way around, but a glance downward told her that her clothing was different, and she felt different in a most uncomfortable way.

At the close of that day, and the following morning, and each day thereafter, she poured out the yearnings of her heart to her Father in heaven, pleading for the ability to be the kind of person worthy of friends—lots of friends, boy friends and girl friends—and making a promise to endeavor to keep all of the commandments in return.

Days and weeks went by. Fall gave way to winter, and while friendships were forming through her sincere respect extended to each student, still there was a need unfulfilled. Then one Sunday afternoon what seemed like an answer to her prayer came. The telephone rang and the voice of one of the special boys at school enthusiastically extended an invitation to her to attend the Sunday movie. Oh, the yearning, the prayers, the

124

promises, the excitement, the conflict, and now the decision. Could this be an answer to her prayers—a Sunday movie? The decision was quickly but painfully made; the invitation was declined, the response cheerful but final. Oh, the torment. Would he ever call again?

A young girl poured out the yearnings of her heart to her Father in heaven, obeyed his commandments, and trusted in the outcome. That particular young man never called again, but in due time her prayers were answered with many friends, boy friends and girl friends, and as that school year drew to a close, she was nominated by the student body to receive a special award for friendliness. Many lessons had been learned that year, but the lesson of greatest importance she expressed in these words:

> Our Father in heaven loves us.
> He knows how we feel.
> He listens to the yearnings of our heart.
> He strengthens us when we're discouraged.
> And he rewards us—in due time.

This same lesson may be yours as you "seek diligently, pray always, and be believing," knowing that your Father in heaven loves you and will guide you as you strive to follow his counsel.

New Era, March 1974, p. 10.

＊——＊

ARDETH G. KAPP

"My Girls Taught Me a Principle of the Gospel"

Some years ago near the close of day something happened in the lives of a group of wonderful young Mia Maid girls. Prior to that afternoon, hours had been spent in cookie making, trying new recipes, program planning, writing new songs, friendship building, and lots and lots of chatting—as I recall, much more chatting than listening. Any observer would agree that was an active activity, but one might also ask, what of the principle being taught?

On the designated day all the plans for delivery of the cookies and presentations of the program were carried out as scheduled amid bubbling laughter, gaiety, and the enthusiasm of youth, everyone wanting to be a part of the action. The only flaw in the plan was that several good-sized bags of cookies were left when all the appointments had been filled. Now the question was, what to do with the extra cookies? And several suggestions came at once, "We could eat them or take them to the Explorers or sell them."

Then the voice of the class president, overriding the rest in a more thoughtful tone, said, "I know what. Let's see if there's an old folks home where grandpas live. They wouldn't have any cookies." A call was made, an immediate appointment arranged, and a group of young girls stood at the front door of a large rest home a little less enthusiastic now about what had seemed like a great idea. The door was opened, and each girl tried awkwardly to push behind the one in front so as not to be first. There was a moment of strain with many thinking, "Why did we come?" Three of the girls quickly unloaded the sacks of cookies on the old table, which appeared to be the only piece of furniture in the room other than the beds and wheelchairs occupied by the patients.

As the girls began singing one of the songs they had prepared in rather hushed tones and with the sweetness of youth, one or two shoulders were raised from a slumped position that had appeared to be permanent. A few patients in wheelchairs were being pushed closer by other patients. The girls continued their songs, gaining a little more courage as the warm response was evident.

At that moment a miracle was taking place. The countenances were gradually but surely changing on the faces of the aged. Expressions were changing and eyes filling with tears as the youths began a different song. This time the others hummed a familiar tune while a foreign exchange student sang the words in German. Only then did a tired bent body slumped on the side of the bed visible through the doorway of an adjoining room raise his head and, in tone soft but audible, join in the words of his native tongue.

Heads were turned, eyes filled with tears, hearts were touched, and lives were changed. A few quiet words of appreciation were expressed, and a different group of young girls walked almost reverently down the steps of that old building. Oh, the thoughts that were shared by each during the trip home! One in an inquiring tone asked, "What happened? I've never felt like this before." And another said, almost in a whisper, "When can we do it again?" My girls and I experienced that day the message spoken of by John, "If any man will do his will, he shall know of the doctrine, whether it be of God, or whether I speak of myself." (John 7:17.) For that moment we were living a principle in a Christlike way, and we all thirsted for more.

When you are in the service of your fellowmen, you are in the service of your God. We were in His service, and we felt His nearness.

ARDETH G. KAPP

"Seek First the Kingdom of God"

May I tell you about Heber, the boy I married. He too was raised on a farm by a widowed mother with nine children. After completing his mission and with no money left, we decided to borrow enough to get married on and begin life together—with two goals: (1) trust in the Lord, and (2) seek first the kingdom of God.

I remember our first visitor—a bill collector from a local mortuary, asking for a back payment on the funeral expenses we had assumed at the death of his mother a few months previously. In this seeming plight, we decided to set some goals, and they included his going to school and my getting a job (by the way, I had never had one other than helping Dad on the farm irrigating and hauling hay and working in a little country grocery store). We decided to dream dreams and think big. It was kind of like a game. My husband said, "Where do you want to work?" And with all the confidence that comes in the privacy of your own little house of dreams, I said, half jokingly, "Samuels," which was at that time considered to be one of the loveliest dress shops in Ogden. He stopped me there and said, "Tomorrow you will go and apply for a job at Samuels; it will be a good experience for you." I've wondered since exactly what he meant.

My heart started to pound at the very thought of riding the bus downtown alone and maybe getting lost. Heber seemed to ignore my sudden anxiety as he began prompting me about how I was to set a goal in my mind to get a job at Samuels and to go in with confidence. Mind you, being the farm boy that he was and well acquainted with poverty, he didn't have much to spare.

The next day as I crossed in front of the beautifully decorated windows with such high-fashioned clothing and I looked down at my homespun dress, my heart sank and my courage departed completely. I hurried to the other side of the street where the challenge seemed a little less threatening. But even there it was too much. I looked down the street to the dime store and thought, I could go there and tell my husband there was no opening at Samuels, but how could I carry the burden of a lie because I was too scared? After crossing the street twice more I faced the store from the other side of the street and finally I just walked across the street, through the front door of Samuels without stopping—trusting in the Lord for courage, but my goal was to just say my speech and get out.

The store was empty. It was early in the morning, and to the first gentleman I saw I nervously gave my speech: "I'm impressed with your store. I know how to work hard and I know I can sell your merchandise." (Under my breath, I said, "Now let me go.")

Mr. Roden, who was dressed in a steel gray flannel suit, stepped back and with a half-smile under his very proper mustache said, "You don't say! Come with me." In the manager's office he said to a very dignified-looking gentleman in a beautifully furnished office, "This young lady says she can sell our merchandise." I've never yet been able to interpret their smiles but Mr. Dye said, "Would you like to begin Monday?" I could hardly wait to tell Heber.

We trusted in the Lord. We dreamed a dream and set a goal. And we both got through school.

And then we dared to dream of having a home, a lovely home, so we set a goal. With no money and no experience in building, but with trust and faith and a specific goal, we began first on paper. We knew nothing about blueprints, but eventually we drew our own plans; then, without the finances to build, the whole idea became an obsession to us, so we built a model to scale from scraps. We set a goal to have a house in two years and build it ourselves. We bought a lot in a beautiful area and we walked across it in the morning, in the evening, in the wind, in the rain, in the fall, and in the winter, and then came the spring.

Heber was called to the high council, and he explained to Elder Spencer W. Kimball, who was the visiting authority dividing the stake, that we planned to build in just one month outside the stake. Elder Kimball just said, "We'll call you, and it will work out." At the end of the month we went to the stake president and explained that we were ready to build and wondered about a release. He just said, "You talk to the Lord about that; it was he who called you." So we went home and talked to the Lord; then we sold the lot. Still, within two years, we had built our home on a more ideal location than we had thought possible within the stake, and had furnished it elegantly. The day the carpet layers finished I sat in the middle of the floor hugging the scraps, with tears rolling down my cheeks. "Seek ye first the kingdom of God and all else shall be added."

And now as I stand about halfway between my horizons, my knowledge of the past assures me without question, with a testimony and a witness, that my horizon yet ahead is as great as the goals I set for myself, if I make myself work toward them.

"You're Like a Mother"

"The stake president sent me to you; he said you'd understand since you don't have any children either." The woman's tone of voice revealed an attitude of resentment as she stood at my front door, and although we were strangers at that moment, I recognized her seeming resentment as a coverup for a troubled and anguished heart. During the several hours that followed, her concerns were spilled out, baring her soul, and her tears flowed freely while she spoke of blessings denied.

She came as a stranger, but sharing deeply personal concerns made us sisters, and I gave silent thanks for the inspiration of the stake president who directed her to my door. Upon leaving she turned, and there was a brief moment of silence as our eyes met; then in a tone of gratitude she said, "The stake president was right, you do understand. Thank you."

As she drove away, I rejoiced in the blessing of being able to see the burden of another, for I did understand. And as I watched her car turn the corner out of sight I was reminded of the words of Elder Neal A. Maxwell at a Brigham Young University fireside: "Every time we navigate safely on this great and narrow way there are other ships that are nearly lost or which are lost which can find their way because of our light."

My path to understanding had not always been one of light; in fact, on occasion there had been much darkness.

As BYU Professor Bruce C. Hafen had once stated: "There are conditions of uncertainty, difficulty, temptations, and insecurity—and yet, they are the very fabric that gives mortality its profound meaning. For only under such conditions is it possible for man to reach enough, search enough, and yearn enough for real growth of the spirit to be possible." But it is possible, and yet there were times over the past years that I really wondered.

I remember a Sunday morning some years ago. Sunday School was a time for rejoicing except on Mother's Day. But I had told myself it would be different this year. The organ music was playing softly as young girls moved quietly down the aisle passing small plants along each row to the mothers who were standing. Last year it was geraniums, this year begonias, and this year I vowed that I would be braver than all the years before. But as the mothers one by one received their small tribute and the girls approached my row, those old familiar feelings returned, and I wished I hadn't come to Sunday School, at least not on Mother's Day.

The little pots in silver wrapping were passed along each row until all the mothers were seated and then, as before, one more plant was passed. And once again I heard the usual whisper, "Go ahead, you deserve it. It's O.K, we've got plenty," and then forcing the little plant into my tightened fist someone whispered, "You're like a mother!"

The meeting ended and my escape through the cultural hall to the back door seemed blocked with unidentifiable objects. I must not cry, I must set a good example, I told myself, especially since my husband was in the chapel carrying out the responsibilities according to his call, showing such genuine concern for others and never thinking of himself. But how could I forget myself when the pounding in my ears, "You're like a mother," seemed to mock the beating of my heart, as my hands resisted the weight of the little begonia.

This year was no different. I thought of the saying "time heals all things," but years were passing and there was no healing, only anguish and heartache. My mind flooded with questions asked too frequently. Were not my eternal companion and I commanded in our sacred temple ceremony to multiply and replenish the earth and to have joy in our posterity? Was there to be no posterity? No joy?

My steps quickened as I hurried to the safety of my own home just a few blocks from the chapel. But even there I found loneliness as I tried to ignore the dinner table set with love and care, but with only two plates.

Another day and I would need to try again, even harder. Weeks later the doorbell rang and a little lad new to the neighborhood looked up with eager eyes, asking, "Can your kids come out and play?" A coldness seemed to creep over me and I almost whispered so no one could hear, "I don't have any." The child in a somewhat questioning tone asked, "Aren't you a mother?" With a quick and somewhat abrupt response my voice replied,

"No, I'm not." The little boy's eyes squinted, and with his head cocked to one side in the innocence of childhood, he asked the question that I had never dared to put into words: "If you're not a mother, what are you?"

Behind the closed door with my back against the wall my whole soul cried out, "Dear God, if I'm not a mother, what am I?" And again the searching question—what was the divine plan for my husband and me and what would the Lord have us do?

Several of our closest and dearest friends had adopted children who had brought the joy of parenthood to their lives. These precious children were in fact their very own through the sealing power of the Holy Priesthood, sealed in an eternal family unit. Together we continued inquiring of the Lord through prayer and fasting and seeking divine guidance as spoken of in Doctrine and Covenants 9:8-9:

"But, behold, I say unto you, that you must study it out in your mind; then you must ask me if it be right, and if it is right I will cause that your bosom shall burn within you; therefore, you shall feel that it is right.

"But if it be not right you shall have no such feelings, but you shall have a stupor of thought. . . ."

But why the stupor of thought when we yearned so for that burning in the bosom, that quiet confirmation that gives assurance of the Lord's will?

We struggled with the desire to experience increased faith that we might receive a positive response to our desired decision, but in our minds we could hear the words, "Whatsoever ye ask the Father in my name it shall be given unto you, that is expedient for you. And if ye ask anything that is not expedient for you, it shall turn unto your condemnation." (D&C 88:64-65.)

Oh, that we might know the Lord's will concerning us!

Like a bird flying through turbulent winds, there were many highs and lows during the coming years and finally, perhaps because of a readiness to receive, the message came. "Trust in the Lord with all thine heart; and lean not unto thine own understanding. In all thy ways acknowledge him, and he shall direct thy paths." (Proverbs 3:5-6.) The words were not new but the message came as an answer to a fervent prayer. "Trust in the Lord." Surely this was the key.

Almost with excitement thoughts came flooding to my mind. Faith in the Lord Jesus Christ—was this not the first principle of the gospel? Faith in a loving father, a divine purpose, an eternal plan. Faith that all things shall come to pass in the due time of the Lord.

I waited anxiously to share these feelings with Heber. I always waited up until he returned from his meetings, even on late nights, because that sharing time had become so special. In a home where a faithful, obedient servant of the Lord endowed with the Holy Priesthood of God honors his priesthood and magnifies his calling, there is a reservoir of limitless power from which to draw strength. This night I would ask for another blessing at the hands of my eternal companion through whom God would speak. And with increased faith we would know God's will concerning us.

Heber had a way of sensing when I needed to talk, and when he arrived home he knew this was one of those times. As we shared our feelings, the quiet hours passed until only the embers were left glowing in the fireplace. Since we had entered into the patriarchal order of celestial marriage, it was possible for a blessing to be pronounced through the power and authority of the priesthood by the natural patriarch in our home. There was a bridge spanned between heaven and earth through priesthood channels, and never again would there be that seeming unquenchable thirst, for we had partaken of living waters.

Guided by this noble man and inspired by the Lord, together we found the direction that would become our purpose for life. We recalled the words of President McKay as we remembered them—the noblest aim in life is to strive to make other lives happy, and then, drawing from the never-ending strength of a righteous companion, I listened to his counsel. "You need not possess children to love them. Loving is not synonymous with possessing, and possessing is not necessarily loving. The world is filled with people to be loved, guided, taught, lifted and inspired."

And finally, together we reread the words of the prophet Joseph Fielding Smith: "If any worthy person is denied in this life the blessings which so readily come to others, and yet lives faithfully and to the best of his or her ability in striving to keep the commandments of the Lord, then nothing will be lost to him. Such a person will be given all the blessings that can be given. The Lord will make up to him the fulness after this life is ended and the full life has come. The Lord will not overlook a single soul who is worthy, but will grant to him all that can be given. . . ." (*Doctrines of Salvation* [Bookcraft, 1955], vol. 2, pp. 176-77.)

I didn't hear Heber's final words as he quietly closed the book; my soul was at peace in slumber, with my head resting on his shoulder.

Things were never quite the same after that. From this source of strength came a quiet peace like the rising of the sun when the warmth of its rays moves upward until it encompasses the entire sky and there are no clouds of darkness in any direction.

This eternal union would be preserved and we would grow toward perfection together as we made a vow to trust in the Lord and his timing knowing "all that my Father hath shall be given unto him." (D&C 84:38.) There would still be questions, but there would also be answers. What do we do in the meantime and what is the purpose of life were the questions I asked the patriarch in our home.

I cannot recall just when it happened, but our cookie jar was just not large enough to contain all the cookies that were dispensed from our door in one day. And so it became a cookie drawer, familiar to the entire neighborhood, young and old. Even the sixteen- and seventeen-year-olds would come, using the excuse, "We need a cookie," in hopes Heber was home with time to listen to them, have fun, and "throw in" a little "fatherly advice," as they called it.

On one occasion when a private conversation seemed to last for hours, I questioned Heber's priorities as they related to a previously planned seemingly important schedule. He nodded his head in understanding of my concern, then thoughtfully responded, "Is anything of greater priority than a young man's life?" I learned never to question his priorities.

My rewards for waiting came at many unexpected times, such as at the grocery store, when the boy bagging my groceries very spontaneously said, "Your husband is a great guy to talk to."

A letter to him from a grateful mother: "Thanks for talking to my boy—it has made all the difference. It's hard without a dad, and now he's decided he wants to go on a mission. Thank you for the time you spend with my son."

One day a little boy brushed past me at the kitchen door, coached by a friend who led the way. "Bradley sez ya get one in both hands," was the comment as his more experienced companion eagerly pulled the cookie drawer wide open for a careful selection. With a concealed smile I responded, "Bradley's right." Once made, the little scavengers bounded from the door with their treasure, and as I stood watching, my heart rejoiced.

A small miracle was beginning to take place. ". . . I give unto men weakness that they may be humble; and my grace is sufficient for all men that humble themselves before me; for if they humble themselves before me, and have faith in me, then will I make weak things become strong unto them." (Ether 12:27.)

An eternal union can be strengthened through seeming adversity, and disappointment can be the foundation for eternal bonds of love and bind a companionship against all the threatening powers that beset the lives of mortals.

Blessings are not denied but sometimes delayed, and it is only in matters of great consequence that souls are bound close together as they reach upward to God. And he is there—". . . lo, I am with you alway, even unto the end of the world. . . ." (Matthew 28:20.)

Years passed swiftly, bringing fulfillment of carefully laid plans as we shared in the joy of seeing the sons of our friends leave for missions and daughters planning for temple marriage and, eventually, that special excitement reserved only for grandparents. While Heber became a power of unwavering strength, on occasion I would experience a fleeting yearning that would each time be quietly softened. At such a time a kind Father in heaven who knows and understands all things put into the mouth of one of his appointed servants during a setting apart blessing those words that would reconfirm and bring to our hearts that "peace that passeth all understanding."

Through the years we have been blessed with boundless opportunities for growth and development—opportunities to serve our fellowmen, young and old, and to rejoice in the gift of life; to see God's handiwork in all that is good; to love deeply and grow spiritually; and to strive to make other lives happy.

It was the week following Mother's Day when, sorting through the mail, I recognized the California return address and rejoiced in another letter from "one of my girls," usually an announcement of an important event, maybe a new little baby. But the message was different this time, like the answer to a long-forgotten prayer:

"I would like to share with you some of the feelings I have at this Mother's Day time. When I was a small girl I can remember other Mother's Days—the passing out of carnations to the mothers in the ward and how special it seemed. Someday I could stand too, perhaps, and be honored along with the rest. This Mother's Day came with special meaning to me as my mind reflected back on a sweet but frail ninety-six-year-old grandmother, the sacrifices and love of my own mother, a sweet mother-in-law who always listens, and now my own tiny special daughter smiling trustingly at her mother's awkward handling.

"But not only did my thoughts reflect back to mothers of blood but to a special, beautiful person who so touched my life as to make me always love and respect her as certainly a mother to me in all the special qualities that go with the word. If you could only know the number of times just thinking of you softened a hardened heart or helped me to my knees when our Heavenly Father's guidance was so needed."

My heart was full to overflowing as my eyes filled with tears of gratitude and blurred my vision so I could read no further. As the tears quietly rolled down my cheeks I thought of the privilege that had been ours to touch in a meaningful way the lives of Jim, Karen, Becky, Paul, Mark, Mindy, Wanda, and many other precious souls we have loved so deeply. And then I reflected on the many lives even yet to be reached and taught, loved, and guided, and a silent prayer escaped my lips: "Thank you, dear God. Truly my cup runneth over. Thou hast allowed thy humble servant to be used as an instrument in thy hands."

With the tears brushed away, I continued reading.

"I love you so very much and I pray often that the Lord's guiding spirit may always be with you so that you can continue to bless the lives of those around you. You're like a mother to me.
Love, Cathie."

MYRTLE WILCOX
KENNINGTON

"She's Alive"

Great was the concern of the little band of pioneers when dysentery spread through the company and little Annie was stricken. "Sister Peterson, the Lord giveth and the Lord taketh away. He has called your baby home. We have delayed too long now. We haven't time to dig a grave, and besides if the Indians found a newly dug grave they would know how recently we have passed here and follow us. Wrap your baby in a blanket and place her under this bush so she cannot be seen, and hurry along," commanded the company leader.

The grief-stricken parents did as they were told and journeyed on. At the night camp, friends tried to console the bereaved couple who had started out with such glorious anticipation for their new land but now had lost not only their newborn son, but also loving, gentle Annie. As the camp members sang that much-loved song, "Come, Come Ye Saints," despair was in her heart and her voice refused to join in. "And if we die before our journey's through . . . all is well! all is well!" One by one the Saints retired to their wagons, leaving Oli and Marn still seated by the campfire.

Suddenly Marn spoke. "Oli, I can't feel that our baby was dead!"

He replied, gently, "I know, dear, we had so many plans, but she was and there is nothing we can do about it but pray that we will be able to raise a family when we settle in Zion. So go to the wagon so you will be refreshed for tomorrow's travel."

Wearily Marn started for the wagon.

"Oli, listen to those wolves, and our baby is lying back there all alone, not even a grave for protection. How can we stand to go on?"

"We must make up our minds to go and trust in the Lord for the rest," he replied.

"I can't, Oli, I can't!" Gently but firmly Oli took her by the arm and led her to their wagon.

Sometime in the early dawn Oli awoke. Marn's place in bed was empty. Fear grasped Oli; he sprang out of bed and ran about the camp frantically calling, "Marn! Marn!" but no answer came. The Saints hurriedly arose and joined the search. Finally, someone shouted, "There she comes." They looked down the long, dusty road they had traveled the day before. Marn, her baby clutched to her breast and stumbling with weariness, was coming down the road toward the camp. Oli ran to meet her, took the tiny girl from her arms, and helped his wife to the campfire. "Darling, why didn't you wake me and tell me you were going back to the baby?" Suddenly a look of astonishment crossed his face. "Our baby, she's alive! She isn't stiff and cold like dead babies are! She's alive!" Eager hands reached for the child and confirmed his statement.

"Brother Peterson, this is a miracle. I was positive your baby was dead yesterday, but she is alive now and a change for the better has come over her. Her sojourn here has not been completed." So saying, the captain walked humbly away to attend to the affairs of the camp.

Kate B. Carter, comp., *Treasures of Pioneer History* (Daughters of the Utah Pioneers), vol. 5, pp. 223-24.

Biographical Sketch

SARAH M. KIMBALL

Sarah M. Kimball was born December 29, 1818, in Phelps, Ontario County, New York, a daughter of Oliver Granger and Lydia Dibble. The wife of Hiram S. Kimball, she was present at the organization of the Relief Society in Nauvoo, Illinois, on March 17, 1842.

She traveled with the Saints to Salt Lake City in 1852 and taught school for several years. In 1857 she was called to be the Relief Society president in the Fifteenth Ward. She was president of the Utah Suffrage Association and a member of the Utah Constitutional Convention in 1882.

Sister Kimball became secretary of the central board of the Relief Society on July 1, 1880, and was called as a counselor in the presidency in 1892. She continued in that calling until her death, December 1, 1898. She was the mother of four sons.

SARAH M. KIMBALL

"After the Pattern of the Priesthood"

Early in the year 1842 Sarah M. Kimball, wife of Hiram Kimball, discussed with a Miss Cook, employed by her as seamstress, about combining their efforts to assist the workers on the Nauvoo Temple. Mrs. Kimball agreed to furnish material if Miss Cook would make shirts for the workmen. Then came the suggestion that the neighborhood women might like to join this effort and form a society for that purpose. The sisters gathered in the parlor of Mrs. Kimball's home and Eliza R. Snow was asked to write a constitution and bylaws to be submitted to the Prophet Joseph Smith for his approval.

When Joseph read Miss Snow's composition he stated it was the best he had ever seen. "But," said he, "this is not what you want. Tell the sisters their efforts are accepted of the Lord, but He has something better for them than a written constitution. Invite them all to meet me and a few of the brethren in the Masonic Hall over at my store next Thursday afternoon, and I will organize the sisters under the priesthood after the pattern of the priesthood. This church will never be perfectly organized until the women are thus organized."

Accordingly, the next Thursday, March 17, 1842, eighteen women gathered in the room over the Prophet's brick store and he organized them into a society. . . .

There were seventeen meetings held by the Relief Society during the first year of its existence. The last meeting, on September 28, 1842, was held in the Grove. The room above Joseph's store had long since become too small, for the membership had grown from 18 to 1,189. At some of these meetings Joseph met with and counseled the sisters. On April 28, 1842, he said:

"Let this Society teach women how to behave towards their husbands, to treat them with mildness and affection. When a man is borne down with troubles, when he is perplexed with care and difficulty, if he can meet a smile instead of an argument or murmur, if he can meet with mildness, it will calm down his soul and soothe his feelings; when a mind is going to despair, it needs a solace of affection and kindness. You will receive instructions through the order of the Priesthood which God has established through the medium of those appointed to lead, guide and direct the affairs of the Church in this last dispensation; and I now turn the key in your behalf in the name of the Lord, and this Society shall rejoice, and knowledge and intelligence shall flow down from this time henceforth; this is the beginning of better days to the poor and needy, who shall be made to rejoice and pour forth blessings on your heads."

Ivan J. Barrett, *Joseph Smith and the Restoration* (Provo, Utah: Brigham Young University Press, August 1970), pp. 426-28.

◆——◆

SARAH M. KIMBALL

"Church Property"

My eldest son was born in Nauvoo, November 22, 1841; when the babe was three days old a little incident occurred which I will mention. The walls of the Nauvoo Temple were about three feet above the foundation. The Church was in need of help to assist in raising the temple walls. I belonged to The Church of Jesus Christ of Latter-day Saints; my husband did not belong to the Church at that time. I wished to help on the temple, but did not like to ask my husband (who owned considerable property) to help for my sake.

My husband came to my bedside, and as he was admiring our three days' old darling, I said, "What is the boy worth?" He replied, "O, I don't know; he is worth a great deal." I said, "Is he worth a thousand dollars?" The reply was, "Yes, more than that if he lives and does well." I said, "Half of him is mine, is it not?" "Yes, I suppose so." "Then I have something to help on the temple." He said pleasantly, "You have?" "Yes, and I think of turning my share right in as tithing." "Well, I'll see about that." Soon after the above conversation Mr. Kimball met the Prophet Joseph Smith, president of the Church, and said, "Sarah has got a little the advantage of me this time; she proposes to turn out the boy as Church property."

President Smith seemed pleased with the joke, and said, "I accept all such donations, and from this day the boy shall stand recorded, *Church* property." Then turning to Willard Richards, his secretary, he said, "Make a record of this, and you are my witness." Joseph Smith then said, "Major [my husband was a major in the Nauvoo Legion], you now have the privilege of paying $500 and retaining possession, or receiving $500 and giving possession." Mr. Kimball asked if city property was good currency, and the President replied that it was. Then said Mr. Kimball, "How will that reserve block north of the temple suit?" President Smith replied, "It is just what we want." The deed was soon made out and transferred to the Church.

President Smith later said to me, "You have consecrated your firstborn son, for this you are blessed of the Lord. I bless you in the name of the Lord God of Abraham, of Isaac, and of Jacob. And I seal upon you all the blessings that pertain to the faithful. Your name shall be handed down in honorable remembrance from generation to generation.

"Your son shall live and be a blessing to you in time, and an honor and glory to you throughout the endless eternities [changes] to come. He shall be girded about with righteousness and bear the helmet and the breastplate of war. You shall be a blessing to your companion, and the honored mother of a noble posterity. You shall stand as a savior to your father's house, and

144

receive an everlasting salvation, which I seal upon you by the gift of revelation and by virtue and authority of the holy priesthood vested in me, in the name of Jesus Christ."

Augusta Joyce Crocheron, comp., *Representative Women of Deseret* (Salt Lake City: J. C. Graham & Co., 1884), pp. 25-26.

MATILDA ROBISON KING*

"You Sing Now"

My grandfather, Thomas Rice King, lived for a time at Cove Fort, Utah. It was during a period of much trouble with the Indians. In 1867 the fort had been built to accommodate ten or twelve families. It was built of stone, with big, thick walls and heavy gates. My grandparents, with other families, lived in this fort for some time while the Indians were on the warpath.

One day the men left the women and children to go into the canyon for a load of wood. As the men didn't expect to be gone very long, and the Indians had not been bothering the families for some time, the gate was left unbolted.

Soon after the men left, several warpainted and vicious-looking Indians stalked through the gate and into the fort. The poor, frightened women caught up their children and hurried to my grandmother's room. The Indians followed them to the door, banged loudly on it, and demanded food. The terror-stricken women did not dare refuse, and so allowed them to enter while they quickly set food on the table. Grandmother was able to con-

*Born in New York in 1811, Matilda Robison, with her husband, Thomas Rice King, joined the Church in 1840. They crossed the plains with their seven children, settling in Fillmore, Utah, where they helped construct first a fort, then the statehouse. In 1876 the King families founded Kingston; then Thomas and Matilda were called to establish the United Order in Piute County. Sister Robison died in 1894.

146

ceal her fright more than the other women. As the warriors started gulping down their food, one of them, who appeared to be their leader or chief, motioned to her and grunted, "You sing now."

Grandmother hesitated, not knowing what to do. She felt she could never control her voice for the fright she felt, hidden though it was. But at the second, more gruff, command, the sisters, fearing for their own and their children's lives, pleaded with her, "Oh, please, Sister King, sing for them." As the Indians began again to grunt, "Hurry up, sing!" she started to sing the first song that came to her mind, hardly realizing that it was a Latter-day Saint hymn, "O Stop and Tell Me, Red Man." After the first verse she paused, but the Indians, who had stopped eating to listen, demanded more. The women were looking at her in astonishment.

When she had sung the entire four verses of the hymn, the Indians, to the amazement and relief of the little group, got up from the table and filed silently out of the door and out of the fort. The women flew to my grandmother. "Why, Sister King, we didn't know you knew the Indian language." Grandmother stared at them. "Know the Indian language? I don't!" "But you sang that entire song in their language," they said excitedly. "That's why they got up and left. They understood every word you sang to them!"

And so she had God's spirit directing her. The message of that hymn went straight to the Indians' hearts, and they left the frightened white people, went back to their camps, and pondered the words of the song.

"And all your captive brothers from every clime shall come
And quit their savage customs, to live with God at home.
Then joy will fill your bosoms and blessings crown your
    days,
To live in pure religion and sing our Maker's praise."

LORENA EUGENIA
WASHBURN LARSEN

"New Shoes for Baby"

In the summer of 1881 my husband was called to go on a mission to Norway, his native land. So we all went to work making preparations for his departure. . . .

In those days money was scarce. To raise money to go on that mission, my husband sold seven acres of land just north of Monroe, Utah, for fifty dollars. He also sold some of the domestic animals. The same land, in no better condition in later years, sold for $200 an acre.

My husband left for that mission in October 1881. At that time I was pregnant, and I had had such a serious time before.

On May 10, 1882, my son Ben Franklin was born. I was very sick from Sunday evening until Wednesday at 1:30 o'clock. My life was despaired of, but by the goodness and mercy of the Lord I was delivered. . . .

I always had a special liking for Sunday School, perhaps because everybody took part.

When the baby was about a year old his shoes wore through on the toes, and soon looked very shabby. I was too proud to take him to church looking shabby. Some people had previously asked me to do velvet painting for them but I had been too busy. However, now, when I was needing shoes for the baby, I sent word that I would do their painting for them, but no work came.

I went to Mother, but there was a lull in dressmaking, and it kept us rustling to get enough money for my husband's missionary expenses. But I knew the Lord could open up a way.

One day when Aunt Julia was sewing at her mother's home, and there was no one at our home but the baby and I, I knelt by his crib and told the Lord that I knew he could help me, that he knew how I longed to attend Sunday School and church, and that it was so hard for me to go and have the baby looking shabby, so would he please inspire someone to send me work so my baby could have new shoes.

I arose and started toward our corral. When I was but a few steps from the house Marie came running and said, "Aunt Lorena, have you any new shoes for baby?" I said no. Then she said, "Aunt Mary Ann told me to run as fast as I could and ask you, and if you haven't, she is going to buy the nicest ones in town for your baby." Next day she sent a beautiful pair of cream morocco shoes trimmed in black.

Autobiography (Brigham Young University Press, 1962), pp. 43ff.

ABIGAIL LEONARD

"I Shall Raise Up a People"

In 1829 Eleazer Miller came to my house for the purpose of holding up to us the light of the gospel and to teach us the necessity of a change of heart. He did not teach creedism, for he did not believe therein. That night was a sleepless one to me, for all night long I saw before me our Savior nailed to the cross. I had not yet received remission of my sins, and in consequence thereof was much distressed. These feelings continued for several days till one day, while walking alone in the street, I received the light of the Spirit.

Not long after this, several associated Methodists stopped at our house, and in the morning while I was preparing breakfast, they were conversing upon the subject of church matters and the best places for church organization. From the jottings of their conversation, which I caught from time to time, I saw that they cared more for the fleece than the flock. The Bible lay on the table nearby, and as I passed I occasionally read a few words until I was impressed with the question: "What is it that separates two Christians?"

For two or three weeks this question was constantly on my mind, and I read the Bible and prayed that this question might be answered to me.

One morning I took my Bible and went to the woods,

where I fell upon my knees and exclaimed: "Now, Lord, I pray for the answer to this question, and I shall never rise till you reveal it to me what it is that separates two Christians." Immediately a vision passed before my eyes, and the different sects passed one after another by me, and a voice called to me, saying, "These are built up for gain."

Then, beyond, I could see a great light, and a voice from above called out: "I shall raise up a people, whom I shall delight to own and bless." I was then fully satisfied and returned to the house.

Not long after this a meeting was held at our house, during which everyone was invited to speak; and when opportunity presented, I arose and said, "Today I come out from all names, sects, and parties, and take upon myself the name of Christ, resolved to wear it to the end of my days."

For several days afterward, many people came from different denominations and endeavored to persuade me to join their respective churches. At length the associated Methodists sent their presiding elder to our house to preach in the hope that I might be converted.

Not long after this, I heard of the Book of Mormon, and on or about the 26th of August, 1831, we were baptized.

Edward W. Tullidge, *The Women of Mormondom* (New York, 1877 [Photo lithographic reprint, Salt Lake City, 1965]), pp. 161-63.

▶━━◀

ABIGAIL LEONARD

"He Was Instantly Healed"

When we heard of the "gathering," we were ready for it and began preparations for the journey. On the 3rd of July, 1832, we started for Jackson County, Missouri, where we arrived sometime in the latter part of December of the same year.

Here we lived in peace and enjoyed the blessings of our religion till the spring of 1833, when the mob came upon us, shed its terror in our midst, and drove us out into the prairie before the bayonet. It was in the cold, cheerless month of November, and our first night's camp was made the thirteenth of that month. The next day we continued our journey over the cold, frozen, barren prairie ground, many of our party barefoot and stockingless, feet and legs bleeding. Mine was the only family whose feet were clothed, and that day, while alone, I asked the Lord what I should do. His answer was: "Divide among the sufferers, and thou shalt be repaid fourfold!" I then gave till I had given more than fifteen pairs of stockings.

In three and a half days from the time of starting, we arrived at a grove of timber, near a small stream, where we encamped for the winter. For a while our men were permitted to return to the settlements in Jackson County, and haul away the provisions they had left behind; but at last our enemies would neither sell to us nor allow us any longer to return for our own provisions left behind.

A meeting was held, and it was decided that but one thing was left to do, which was to return to Jackson County, to the place we had recently been forced to leave. This we did, and on the evening of February 20, 1834, soon after our arrival in the old deserted place, we went to meeting and returned home. It was about eleven o'clock at night, while we were comfortably seated around a blazing fire built in an old-fashioned Dutch fireplace, when someone, on going out, discovered a crowd of men at a little distance from the house, on the hill. This alarmed the children, who ran out, leaving the door open. In a moment or two, five armed men pushed their way into the house and presented their guns to my husband's breast, and demanded, "Are you a Mormon?"

My husband replied, "I profess to belong to the Church of Christ."

They then asked if he had any arms, and on being told that he had not, one of them said, "Now, you, walk outdoors!" My husband was standing up and did not move.

Seeing that he would not go, one of them laid down his gun, clutched a chair, and dealt a fierce blow at my husband's head.

Fortunately, the chair struck a beam overhead, which turned and partially stopped the force of the blow, and it fell upon the side of his head and shoulder with too little force to bring him down, yet enough to smash the chair in pieces upon the hearth. The fiend then caught another chair, with which he succeeded in knocking my husband down beneath the stairway. They then struck him several blows with a chairpost upon the head, cutting four long gashes in the scalp. The infuriated men then took him by the feet and dragged him from the room. They raised him to his feet, and one of them, grasping a large boulder, hurled it with full force at his head; but he dropped his head enough to let the stone pass over, and it went against the house like a cannonball. Several of them threw him into the air and brought him, with all their might, at full length upon the ground. When he fell, one of them sprang upon his breast and, stamping with all his might, broke two of his ribs.

They then turned him upon his side and with a chairpost dealt him many severe blows upon the thigh, which were heard at a distance of one hundred and twenty rods. Next they tore off his coat and shirt and proceeded to whip him with their gunsticks. I had been by my husband during this whole affray, and one of the mob, seeing me, cried out, "Take that woman in the house!" Four of them presented their guns to my breast, and jumping off the ground with rage and uttering the most tremendous oaths, they commanded me to go into the house. This order I did not obey, but hastened to my husband's assistance, taking stick after stick from them, till I must have thrown away twenty.

By this time my husband felt that he could hold out no longer, and raising his hands toward heaven, asking the Lord to receive his spirit, he fell to the ground, helpless. Every hand was stayed, and I asked a sister who was in the house to assist me in carrying him indoors.

We carried him in, and after washing his face and making him as comfortable as possible, I went forth into the mob and reasoned with them, telling them that my husband had never harmed one of them nor raised his arm in defense against them. They then went calmly away, but next day circulated a report that they had killed a Mormon.

After the mob had gone, I sent for the elder, and he, with two or three of the brethren, came and administered to my husband, and he was instantly healed. The gashes on his head grew

153

together without leaving a scar, and he went to bed comfortable. In the morning he was so well that he went with me to meeting that same day.

Tullidge, *The Women of Mormondom*, pp. 163-67.

NELDA PIERSON
LITCHFIELD

"Mrs. Pleasant"

I shall call her "Mrs. Pleasant," be-
cause I think of her when I hear that adjective. We met many
years ago, when my husband and I had been married for only a
few months. An older man with whom my husband worked at
the office invited us to his home for dinner. The remarks of this
man's lovely wife made an indelible impression on my mind.
The dinner was a veritable feast; yet, I remember less about it.

As I helped with the dishes, my eyes lingered on the
"Thursday" pattern I was holding, and I remarked about the
beauty of the hand-worked towel.

"Oh, that was the poorer one," she said. "I think we just
have some 'Thursdays' and 'Mondays' left. The children like the
other designs better."

She took me with her into the boys' rooms while she got the
small children into their pajamas and sent them into the bathrooms for their baths and to brush their teeth. She seemed well-
organized, loving, and very patient, and her children responded
with sincere devotion. When they were both clean and dressed,
they appeared in the hall, ready for the session of what their
mother called "horseplay." Mrs. Pleasant maintained that all
tiny folks needed to be tired and happy before bedtime. She
allowed them one-half hour in the playroom at the end of the

bath session, timing them by the clock. I noted that she had a cupboard up high in the room in which she kept first-aid supplies. I watched the twinkle in her eyes when she admitted that these supplies were sometimes useful after a nightly workout.

"My husband and I feel that the children need to play 'roughhouse' now and then," she said, smiling.

When the little boys were tucked down into their beds, she said we could have a good talk. Our husbands were in the den, and the older children were busy in the dining room doing their homework. We went back to the playroom. The comfort of the children had been paramount in the planning of that room. Mrs. Pleasant stated that it had taken five years to complete this room to specifications. Rocking horses, painted floor games, basketball equipment, and an extensive children's library of books and musical recordings made the room a haven of fun. There was a noticeable lack of dolls and girls' toys, of course, since the Pleasants had no daughters.

I stood in awe at the material blessings that had been bestowed upon the Pleasant children. Their mother, a cultured university graduate, sat down on one of the lounges beside me and sighed, "You know, dear, we were not always able to buy such furnishings as we have now." Little by little, she shared the details with me.

"My father was a doctor, and my husband's people had a successful business. They felt there was no reason for us to live in the 'cubbyhole' we rented. However, we wanted to feel independent. It's true, we had quite a struggle while my husband was getting through college; the only money we had was what I could earn as secretary to the dean of engineering."

The tiny suite in which they lived was close to the campus, and this later saved transportation expenses. The two of them learned to budget realistically. They took year-end inventory to decide on purchases for the future. In allowing themselves few luxuries, they were able to start a small savings account in the bank. They had two rules in those days: first, only one movie or dance a month, and second, dessert once a week, usually on Sunday.

"When you look at our home now, you, I realize, can hardly believe that once we got by with apple-box cupboards— apple boxes were free from our grocery store. I made attractive drapes for the boxes from very inexpensive print, bought as a remnant. In the fall and spring, I would rent a sewing machine for a week, to keep things in good condition and myself clothed. For the five-dollar fee, I could sew what I needed. I can see that little portable now, on top of our dresser. Oh, we called it a dresser, although it was simply another set of apple boxes, draped, with a mirror on top. Every inch of space in that apartment-room was at a premium."

She told of an incident that indicated clearly the dimensions of the room.

"One night, when we had both gone to sleep, Mother knocked at our door. It was after midnight, and since we had no phone, she had come to bring us the news of Uncle David's accident. She said that Father was working on him in the operating room. By the time I had awakened my husband and we had lifted the bed up into the wall closet, in order to open the door, Mother seemed upset, and we heard her grumble, 'To think that an only child, a daughter of mine, would have to live like this!' You see, she often forgot the early challenges of her marriage, when Father was attending medical school."

The night of our visit, Mrs. Pleasant summed up her thoughts with the remark that all women ought to learn to enjoy what they can afford to own.

Last week, a young married woman came to my home, obviously disturbed because she did not have some of the worldly appliances that my husband, after years of planning, had provided for our family. I felt impressed to tell her about Mrs. Pleasant. My friend had complained, "Why, you should see our apartment! It is no bigger than the office where I used to work as a receptionist before our marriage. I am ashamed to invite anyone to our place."

A letter came in my mailbox today from her. She climaxed her remarks with these comments: "Too many of us young wives are not willing to sacrifice while our husbands are getting started. We expect now what our mothers have taken a lifetime to have. We need more Mrs. Pleasants! She has made me happy, once again, to live out of our suitcases and cardboard boxes. Thank you for letting me meet her!"

Relief Society Magazine, January 1968, pp. 43-45.

ANNA MAESER*

"Here's the Fifty Cents You Gave Me"

My husband [Karl G. Maeser] continued to labor in many capacities until the April conference in 1867, when he was called on a mission to Germany and Switzerland.

The custom was in those days to read the list of names of missionaries from the stand at general conference, generally at the last session of the conference. No one had been previously notified, and so these appointments came as a complete surprise.

His journal records that he left home for Europe with Brother Octave Ursenbach on May 10, 1867. He wrote:

"I cast, at the mouth of Emigration Canyon, my last look back to the City I love so well, wishing, as a farewell benediction to my people, that they should become in strength and independence as their mountains; in loveliness and beauty like their valleys and in purity to resemble their clear atmosphere, transmitting, unbroken and undiminished, the rays from the Source of Light.

"The first night camp terminated my home life, and with

---

*Anna Maeser was married June 11, 1854, in Neustadt, Germany, to Karl G. Maeser. After joining the Church, they immigrated to Utah, where Brother Maeser later became a prominent Utah educator and was president of Brigham Young University. Sister Maeser died April 2, 1896.

the waking hours next morning, commenced that great journey which should carry me across the continent, the Atlantic, through several countries of Europe, until, after some years, I might return again to my dear mountain home. When I left home, I gave my wife, Anna, a fifty-cent 'shin plaster,' which was all the money I had at that time. She told me that she would give me that 'shin plaster' back on my return."

Three years later, when he returned, I did not go to the depot to meet him, but waited in joyful expectancy for his home-coming. There had been something doing in that home during the last few months—a new "store carpet," new chairs, lace curtains, lambrequins, all paid for, which furnished the front room. As Karl came up the front walk, I stepped out on the portico; he paused to look at me, and I called to him, "Here's the fifty cents you gave me, and another one besides."

He entered the door of his own home once more, stretched out his hands, and exclaimed, "Thank God, it is accomplished; I have done my duty, and my dear Heavenly Father has brought me safe home again. His great name be praised." A fine supper had been prepared, and a happy family gathered around the board. Before retiring, some very fervent prayers of gratitude for father's and husband's safe return ascended to the Throne of Grace.

Karl G. Maeser, pp. 48-51, 72.

EMMA RAY RIGGS McKAY*

"Are You Sure You Want Me?"

Ray was about eighteen when her mother called to her one day to look out of the front room window. Joining her mother, she was impressed by what she saw. Two tall, handsome young men, each holding an arm to help their mother up the walk, were accompanied by their two younger sisters.

"See, Ray, how attentive the boys are to their mother. They will make fine husbands for some fortunate girls someday." While attending the University of Deseret, these young people were to be tenants of her mother's home for the next two years and were to be numbered among Ray's best friends. Little did she realize then that six years hence, the dear friends would be her brother and sisters, and David O. McKay, the dearest one of all, her beloved, lifelong companion.

Ray, too, was attending the University of Deseret. One day as she was walking down a corridor she heard someone speaking. Noticing the door of the room ajar, she stood in the hallway and

*Emma Ray Riggs McKay was born on June 23, 1877, in Salt Lake City. On January 2, 1901, she was married to David O. McKay, who later became the ninth President of the Church. She served in the auxiliaries of the Church and was a remarkable wife and mother. Sister McKay died November 14, 1970, in Salt Lake City, at the age of 93.

160

listened to a talk given by young David O. McKay before the Normal Society.

That young man will amount to something someday, she thought to herself.

In June 1897, David O. McKay, president of his class, was graduated from the Normal School and was chosen to be the valedictorian. During the commencement exercise, Ray, thrilled by his words, wondered whether she would ever see him again. She was overjoyed when, in July of that same year, his sisters, Jeannette and Ann McKay, invited her to Huntsville to attend David O.'s missionary farewell, and she willingly accepted. That evening after the program David O. walked Ray from the chapel to the McKay home, holding her hand all the way. They agreed to correspond while he was away.

Just before he was released from his mission, David O. received an appointment by mail to teach at the Weber Stake Academy in Ogden, which he readily accepted. The courtship that had begun at his missionary farewell blossomed through correspondence and was continued in earnest for a year and a half after he returned from Scotland in August 1899.

One colorful autumn afternoon under a graceful umbrella tree, he proposed to her in Lester Park in Ogden. She was thrilled but answered, "Are you sure you want me?"

"Yes. I am very sure," smiled her sweetheart.

They became engaged. It was some months later, January 2, 1901, when David O. called for Ray in his horse-drawn hack to drive her three blocks to the Salt Lake Temple. Here they were married by Elder John Henry Smith to be companions for eternity.

Relief Society Magazine, June 1967, pp. 409-11.

Biographical Sketch

Jennette Evans McKay was born near Merthyr-Tydfil, South Wales, on August 23, 1850, a daughter of Thomas and Margaret Powell Evans. Her parents were converted to The Church of Jesus Christ of Latter-day Saints that year, and six years later they immigrated to Utah, settling in Ogden.

On April 9, 1867, Jennette was married to David McKay in the Endowment House in Salt Lake City, with Wilford Woodruff officiating. They settled in a log cabin in Huntsville, Utah, where they reared their family of four sons and four daughters (two other daughters died in infancy). Her oldest son and third child was David Oman McKay, who became president of the Church in 1951. Another son, Thomas E., served as an Assistant to the Council of the Twelve.

Jennette McKay was always an inspiration and strength to her family. When her husband was called on a mission to Scotland in 1881, she insisted that he go, though it meant she would be left with the responsibilities of the farm and the family, and a new baby was born just ten days after his departure. However, she managed to keep her two sons in school, organized the farmwork and household chores, and even made additions to their home during his absence.

In 1961 President McKay visited his mother's birthplace at Merthyr Tydfil, Wales, and placed a plaque on the four-room cottage where she was born. Two years later he dedicated a chapel there, and an organ that had been presented to him in his mother's honor by a group of Salt Lake City businessmen was installed.

JENNETTE EVANS McKAY

"The Greatest Miracle"

When David O. McKay was eight years of age, his father, David, received a call to go on a mission. To accept such a call for two or three years away from home was no easy decision to make. Another baby was on its way, and plans had been made to enlarge the house and furnishings. The responsibilities of running the farm were too great to be left to his wife, so when David showed the letter calling him to a mission, he said; "Of course it is impossible for me to go." Jennette read the letter, looked at her husband, and said decisively, "Of course you must accept; you need not worry about me. David O. and I will manage things nicely!" Even though many of the neighbors and friends took the side of David and maintained that this was an inopportune time for him to leave home, Jennette stood firm. "Well," said Uncle John Grow to David, "you may be right, and you may be wrong; but if Jennette has set her mind that you should answer the mission call, you might as well give in! I'll keep an eye on things and help out when I can."

On April 19, 1881, David O.'s father left for his mission in Scotland, leaving young David with new responsibilities. David O. had the normal vitality of youth, as evidenced by his aunt's statement while she was taking care of him as a youngster: "Jennette, if you will just take care of this boy, I'll gladly cook for the threshers!" In the absence of his father, the boy quickly redirected his energies to chores and farm work. Circumstances thus helped to produce a maturity beyond his physical years.

He was proud of his new baby sister, Annie, and realized that added responsibilities now rested on his shoulders. With the help of members of the priesthood quorums, the grain was planted, and the summer brought a good crop of hay. The fall brought a disappointment, however, because prices of grain were too low to bring a profit. Upon good advice the grain was stored until spring when a high price was obtained. Without sending word to her husband, Jennette decided to surprise him by having the addition to the house built. On the eve of his return, the family sat around the living room to hear some of his experiences. One of the children asked if he had had any miracles. He put his arm around his wife and replied, "Your mother is the greatest miracle that one could ever find!"

Llewelyn R. McKay, *Home Memories of President David O. McKay* (Deseret Book Co., 1956), pp. 5-6.

JENNETTE EVANS McKAY

"Mother Loved Us"

As told by President David O. McKay

I cannot think of a womanly virtue that my mother did not possess. Undoubtedly many a youth, in affectionate appreciation of his mother's love and unselfish devotion, can pay his mother the same tribute; but I say this in the maturity of manhood when calm judgment should weigh facts dispassionately. To her children, and all others who knew her well, she was beautiful and dignified. Though high-spirited, she was even-tempered and self-possessed. Her dark brown eyes immediately expressed any rising emotion which, however, she always held under perfect control.

In the management of her household she was frugal yet surprisingly generous, as was Father also, in providing for the welfare and education of her children. To make home the most pleasant place in the world for her husband and children was her constant aim, which she achieved naturally and supremely. Though unselfishly devoted to her family, she tactfully taught each one to reciprocate in little acts of service.

Her soul, to quote the words of the poets, was 'As pure as lines of green that streak the first white of the snowdrop's inner leaves.' In tenderness, watchful care, loving patience, loyalty to home and to right, she seemed to me in boyhood, and she seems to me now after these years, to have been supreme.

Mother left us when she was still young, only fifty-four. During the intervening twenty-seven years I have often wished that I had told her in my young manhood that my love for her and the realization of her love and of her confidence gave me power more than once during fiery youth to keep my name untarnished and my soul from clay.

From my beautiful, ever devoted, and watchful mother, from my loyal sisters in our early home associations, and from my beloved wife during the maturer years that followed I have received my high ideals of womanhood. No man has had inspiration from nobler, more loving women. To them I owe a debt of eternal gratitude.

Among my most precious soul treasures is the memory of Mother's prayers by the bedside, of her affectionate touch as she tucked the bedclothes around my brother and me and gave each a loving, good-night kiss. We were too young and roguish then to appreciate such devotion fully, but not too young to know that Mother loved us.

It was this realization of Mother's love, with loyalty to the precepts of an exemplary father, which more than once during youth turned my steps from the precipice of temptation.

If I were asked to name the world's greatest need, I should say unhesitatingly wise mothers; and second, exemplary fathers.

If mother love were but half rightly directed, and if fatherhood were but half what it should be in example and honor, much of the sorrow and wickedness in the world would be overcome.

The home is the source of our national life. If we keep the spring pure, we shall have less difficulty in protecting the stream from pollution.

Millennial Star, September 1963, pp. 222 ff.

MARILYN McMEEN MILLER*

"The Greatest Privilege"

On my way to church one Sunday morning I saw a group of boys playing ball on the schoolground. Dressed in ragged jeans and shirts, they were screaming and pounding their fists with excitement as one of the team members crossed the goal line. It looked like a good game—a wonderful activity for any other day except Sunday.

I knew several of these boys. They were from Latter-day Saint homes. But they were missing out on one of the greatest blessings of their lives—the privilege of going to church. They probably thought of church as a restriction or a burden, not a privilege.

I remembered back to the time when I had felt that way. But there came a special period in my life when I learned what a privilege it is to be a Latter-day Saint.

When I was a child in Junior Sunday School, I was not much concerned about keeping the Sabbath day holy or about taking on many of the responsibilities my family had accepted when we became members of The Church of Jesus Christ of

*Marilyn McMeen Miller, a daughter of William O. and Lola Francis Miller, was born in Denver, Colorado. After graduating from Brigham Young University, she went on to receive her master's degree, then taught English at BYU for seven years. The author of three books, Sister Miller presently is an editor at the BYU Press. She has served in the Sunday School and Relief Society.

Latter-day Saints. I liked going with my parents to be sealed in the temple, and I liked Primary. But I didn't like the long meetings and having to give talks and to fast and to pay tithing.

At the time my baby brother was born, we lived in a non-Mormon community near downtown Denver, Colorado. Our three-story, middle-class brick home was in an unusual spot, not far from two extreme levels of society—the slums to the north and the mansions of the wealthy across the park.

I was so eager to make friends with the wealthy children who lived in those beautiful homes across the park that I couldn't think of anything else. When a little girl from one of these homes invited me to come over one Sunday so her parents could take us to their ranch to ride horses, I was wild with excitement. I didn't even think about missing Sunday School. How disappointed I was when my mother reminded me that I had promised to give the sacrament gem in Junior Sunday School that morning!

Why did I have to go to church? Why did I have to give the sacrament gem? Why didn't any of my other friends have to go to church or pay tithing or fast or give talks? Before we were members of the Church we could do as we pleased. I resented the restrictions placed upon me now.

My mother was wise and kind. She said briefly, "You don't want to miss church. It is one of the greatest privileges you have."

I did not see it that way. But when I called my friend, she said they would be going to the ranch on Sunday afternoons for a while. If I was free, I should drop over some other Sunday.

During the next week my baby brother was born, and my mother became gravely ill. She lay in the hospital near death for a number of days.

In the evenings we three girls would play out on the porch in the gathering twilight, walking the railing and listening to the sounds of the hundreds of cars pounding and spinning their tires over the pavement, waiting for my father to come home. When he arrived, his face was always drawn and worn. Each time we listened breathlessly to his reports of Mother's condition. It was always the same—critical.

The next Sunday afternoon arrived. Hesitantly I dressed in my boots and jeans and looked out toward the park from my window for Father's return from the hospital. Finally I saw him walk slowly across the lawn to the house.

"How's Mama?" we whispered, afraid to ask.

My father did not speak for a moment. "If Heavenly Father takes her," he finally reasoned slowly, "we must have faith that it is the right decision."

"Will Mama go away for good?" my sister asked.

My father took my sister in his arms and said, "Your mama will never go away for good. That is why we are fortunate in being Latter-day Saints. We were sealed as a family in the temple, and that means Mother will always be with us. She may go to visit Heavenly Father for a while, but all of us will always be together." I could see tears glistening in his eyes. "We are so blessed by Heavenly Father and by the privilege of belonging to his church."

At that moment I remembered my mother's smiling eyes and her gentle smile. Then I seemed to hear her words, "You don't want to miss church. It is one of the greatest privileges you have."

I raced upstairs and got out of my boots and jeans and into my Sunday clothes.

That evening as I took the sacrament, I said a silent prayer of thanks to my Heavenly Father that I was there, that I had the privilege of taking the sacrament, that I had the privilege of being a Latter-day Saint so I could always stay with my family.

I never prayed so hard in my life as I did that week. Night after night beside my narrow bed I talked to my Heavenly Father and promised him that I would go to sacrament meeting and pay my tithing. I promised him that I would try to be a good Latter-day Saint if only he would let my mother live.

We were blessed, and my mother's life was spared. But I was doubly blessed, for I also learned how fortunate I was to be a Latter-day Saint and to have the privilege of going to church.

Instructor, July 1969, pp. 236-37.

CAROLINE EYRING
MINER*

"Wearing a Face into a Mother's"

Today as the college graduating class filed past the audience, a hand waved frantically in an attempt to attract one of the graduates. It was a mother's work-blunted hand, and as I looked at her more closely, her withered face beaming with pride and happiness, I suddenly knew what Gulbransen meant when he used in one of his books the striking phrase, "wearing a face into a mother's."

How does a mother's face get the mother-look of love and pride, forgiveness, faith, and trust that we all know? It is worn there day by day as a great painting is made, stroke by stroke. To a fresh, young creature whose face is classically fair and lovely, a child is born, and with its birth there come into the fair young face faint lines of a great unselfish love that has borne pain and sorrow for another. In the years that follow there come more children, more cares, more tears, more sacrifices, and the fair young face wears, line by line, and love-stroke by love-stroke, into the face of a mother.

°Caroline Eyring Miner was born in Colonia Juarez, Mexico, to Edward Christian and Caroline Cottam Romney Eyring. She was reared in Arizona and attended school there as well as at Brigham Young University. She and her husband, Glen Miner, have eight children. Sister Miner was an English teacher for thirty years and served on the YWMIA general board twenty years. The author of seven books as well as scores of poems, stories, and articles, she was Utah Mother of the Year in 1973.

Not all mother faces are weathered and prematurely discolored and wrinkled; those are not the really telling marks of a mother face, but are the signs of a life struggle on the part of an individual whether she is a mother or not. The lines on a mother's face that make it distinctly a mother's face are those that gather about her mouth as she says, as she has said a hundred times, "Child, you didn't mean it, and I love you more than life in spite of all."

Relief Society Magazine, February 1949, p. 97.

ANNIE EMMA DEXTER
NOBLE

"This Is the Way, Walk Ye in It"

I was born on the 15th of February in the little English village of Friezland, near the city of Nottingham, in the year 1861.

My parents had thirteen children, six girls and seven boys. I was the tenth child.

Abraham and I were married and we had five lovely daughters. In the year 1906 my husband became very ill. The doctor ordered a rest from his work, so we went to Gainsborough to visit some friends. One afternoon while we were there, two gentlemen called and, to my great surprise, I learned that they were "Mormons." Almost as soon as I knew who they were, I felt a great desire to hear something of their beliefs. Question after question I put to them, and they answered each one to my entire satisfaction. The scriptures were opened to me in a manner I had never known before. My husband, not feeling well, took no part in the conversation, and neither did the other members of the household, but they listened attentively.

After two weeks of complete rest, my husband felt very much improved, and he went back to work. It was not long, however, before he had a relapse. Again the doctor prescribed a rest, and a sea voyage was decided upon. We decided to visit some friends in Brooklyn, New York. It was a very sad time for us all. We left our dear children in the care of my husband's two maiden sisters and sailed from Liverpool on January 22, 1907.

When we left England we thought three months' change would fully restore my husband's health, but seven months passed and we realized that he was not yet well enough to hold his position. One morning I was alone in my bedroom. I was unusually troubled and I knelt down and poured out my feelings to my Father in heaven. I asked him to make known to me whether or not my husband would recover, and promised him that if he would spare his life, we would devote our lives to his service.

I had no sooner uttered the prayer than a voice spoke these words: "Your husband shall be made completely well and he shall preach the gospel." I stood up, amazed, but full of joy. I knew without a doubt that my husband would be made well and strong again. But the second promise puzzled me greatly. I finally came to the conclusion that he was to enter college and prepare for the Baptist ministry. Such an idea as Mormonism had never seriously entered my mind.

From that time my husband began to get better. A month later we were homeward bound. My heart was full of hope and joy at the prospect of seeing our beloved children, and the precious assurance that God would fulfill his promise made us equal to the many trials that came our way for long months after.

Eighteen months passed, and still there was no sign that the second promise would be fulfilled. One day, as I was preparing dinner, a knock came to our door. I answered it. A young man asked me if I would accept a gospel tract. I quickly turned it over and saw the words *Church of Jesus Christ of Latter-day Saints*. I told him that I had met some of his people two years before and that I had hoped ever since to hear more of their teachings. Every week after that the elders visited our home, explaining the principles of the gospel. Two years passed away and no elder had mentioned the subject of baptism.

One day the thought came to me that I could not expect to go on forever taking up the valuable time of these young men, and if I believed the truths that they were teaching, I should be baptized. This was a most disturbing thought to me. I was afraid to discuss my feelings with my husband, for he was not particularly interested in the gospel. I became unhappy and ill at ease. I felt more and more that I could not go on with Mormonism; that meant that I must give it up—and oh, how dreadful it would be to give it up! Soon after, when Elder Brown came, he saw at once that something was wrong. He asked me if I were unhappy and I answered feverishly, "Yes, I am wretched. I feel I cannot go on any longer with Mormonism. I must give it up or accept it."

He stood up before me and in a most decided manner told me that the time had come for me to be baptized. I answered bitterly, "But I have already been baptized."

He said, "Have you been baptized by one having authority?" I hung my head and could not answer. Then without another word he put out his hand and said, "Good afternoon, Mrs. Noble," and was quickly gone.

How dreadful I felt and how alone. I went immediately to my room and dropped to my knees and cried out, "Father, I am ignorant and cannot see the way; tell me whether this is the true church or not."

Instantly I heard these words, "This is the way, walk ye in it." That was all, but it was enough. No words of mine can express the convincing power that came into my whole being, and with it came peace. I stood up and said, "Now I know beyond a doubt."

It took me three weeks to get enough courage to ask my husband to allow me to be baptized. One night after my husband had put out the light and we were in bed, I told myself that I could not wait any longer, so I tried to make my voice natural and softly asked, "Abe, would you mind very much if I were baptized into the Mormon Church?"

I felt him start, and then came his answer, "No, I don't think I would. I have seen this coming and I know what kind of woman you are. You have not come to this decision in a hurry and if I could keep you from it, I would not dare. I dare not come between you and God."

Never have I forgotten the deep love that I felt for him at that moment, and I felt sure that God would show to him also that Mormonism was true.

I was baptized by Elder Brown on Saturday, November 5, 1910. My daughter Julia was baptized the Sunday following.

Fifteen months after I joined the Church, my husband and my daughter Dora were baptized. A few days following his baptism, my husband was deeply impressed to go to Utah, although just before his baptism he had expressed his unwillingness to leave his own country. Three months later we were on our way. We immigrated to Utah and settled in Ogden. There the last member of our family of five was baptized. We were happy in our new home and made many friends, and each of us tried to do what was asked of us in the Church.

We had lived in Ogden eight years when my husband and I were called on a mission to England. When the call came my mind went back to that day so long ago when a voice spoke to me and said, "Your husband shall be made well and shall preach the gospel." For more than twenty-five years I had waited for the fulfillment of the second promise, and at last it was fulfilled; my husband was called to preach the gospel. I felt like singing all day long, for truly the Lord had manifest his power unto us. We fulfilled a mission in England among our friends and relatives and we rejoice that we had the opportunity to help in the work of the Lord. Our only desire is to do his gracious will and be faithful to the end.

Mary Pratt Parrish, *Supplement to the Seagull, Home Builder Lesson Book* (General Board of the Primary Association of The Church of Jesus Christ of Latter-day Saints, 1951), pp. 47-52.

ANNIE EMMA DEXTER NOBLE

"Go and Look in the Little Jewel Box"

It was my practice before my husband joined the Church to pay my tithing on my monthly allowance that he gave me to keep up the house, but since he did not yet believe in the law of tithing, I did not tell him about this.

One month I ran short and had to ask for some extra money.

He looked surprised and rebuked me, saying, "You must learn to cut your coat according to your cloth."

This hurt me terribly and I decided that I would never again ask him for extra money. I worked hard to make ends meet so that I would have enough to pay my tithing. But try as I would, I found it very difficult, and once again several months later I faced the same problem. I did not have enough money to finish out the month.

When I was trying to decide what to do, I suddenly found myself complaining that the Lord expected too much of us when he asked for a tenth. This questioning of his demands only lasted a moment or two and then a feeling of deep remorse came over me for having had such a thought. Immediately I knelt down before the chair that stood by the cupboard and asked the Lord to forgive me for my ingratitude, for I truly felt that I had received from his hands a "pearl of great price," and for me to begrudge a paltry tenth to him was indeed inexcusable. I begged him to forgive me, and with tears streaming down my face I promised him that I would never again question the law of tithing.

After I had asked the Lord's forgiveness I began to wonder what I should do. I was very sad that day, for I still felt that I could not ask my husband for more money. It was Tuesday, and on that evening, we always had a cottage meeting at the home of Brother and Sister Harrison. I was especially happy to go there that night, for their home had always been to me like a haven in a storm at sea. There I was safe from the frowns and disapprovals of all my friends and relatives. As I went upstairs to dress for the meeting, I still felt very sad and troubled. I knelt down and prayed that the Lord would take from me this troubled feeling so that I could enjoy the cottage meeting. Just as I finished my prayer, I heard these words: "Go and look in the little jewel box in the back of your drawer."

I quickly obeyed and hastily took out the jewel box and opened it. There lay side by side two bright sovereigns. Needless to say, I was amazed and so filled with joy that I recall that I had the sensation of walking on air as I went to the meeting. The sovereign at that time was equal to a five-dollar gold piece in American money.

Supplement to the Seagull, Home Builder Lesson Book, 1951, pp. 50-51.

◄——◆——►

"The Three Notes"

I was asked at one time to substitute for the organist at union [leadership] meetings for the next six months. It was the custom to have five minutes of music before the meeting started.

Before I left home one Sunday, I felt a great desire to play a piece called "Le Jet d'Eau," which meant "The Jet of Water." This was a piece that I had learned many years before but I no longer had the music. Before I left home I tried to play it, but when I came to a certain chord, I could not remember the notes. I tried again, but I still could not remember the three notes that made that one chord. I felt sure that I could remember and so I tried again, but again I stopped at the same place; so I decided to play something else.

While I was sitting, waiting for the stake president to tell me to commence the music, I again felt a great desire to play that particular piece and offered a silent prayer that the chord would be shown to me. Immediately I envisioned in my mind a keyboard, and the three notes that I wanted stood out from the rest.

I am ashamed to confess that when I started to play, I did not have the courage to play that piece, but played another one instead; but when I reached home, I at once put my fingers on those keys that had been shown me and sure enough, they were the right ones. I have often wondered what my Father in heaven thought of my lack of faith, and wished I had trusted in him enough to try that piece at union meeting that day.

Supplement to the Seagull, Home Builder Lesson Book, 1951, pp. 51-52.

Biographical Sketch

If one phrase could describe Stella Harris Oaks's life it would be the "second mile." Her family, community, and professional accomplishments clearly reflect the extra strength, extra wisdom, and extra courage she has said are necessary to go the second mile.

Born in Provo, Utah, Sister Oaks received her elementary and high school education in Payson, Utah, and was graduated with a Bachelor of Arts degree from Brigham Young University. On June 14, 1929, she was married to Lloyd E. Oaks and accompanied him to Philadelphia to complete his senior year in medical school. Within a few years, however, at the height of his career, Dr. Oaks was stricken with tuberculosis, from which he died in June 1940. With the intense faith that has been characteristic of her life, Stella Oaks undertook to prepare herself for the dual role of father and mother for her three young children, then ages eight, four, and one. She obtained a master's degree from Columbia University and began a career of teaching and service.

Family life education in the state of Utah and the Church has commanded much of Sister Oaks's attention. She is founder of Brigham Young University's Family Life Conference and headed adult education in the Provo School District for twenty-four years. In 1960 she was Timpanogos District Mother of the Year. She has served as director of education for senior citizens in Provo and president of the Provo Mental Health and Child Guidance Committee. At present she serves on the Utah State Advisory Committee of the Council on Aging. Sister Oaks has served two terms on the Provo City Council and as assistant and acting mayor of Provo. The local newspaper often refers to her as Provo City's mother.

Stella Oaks's second-mile endeavors in the Church include serving as BYU Fourth Stake Relief Society president for eight years and as a member of the MIA general board. She is in great demand as a speaker and has been a featured attraction at Education Week and Education Day programs throughout the Church.

Notable evidence of the effectiveness of Mrs. Oaks's efforts as father and mother are the achievements of her children. Dallin H. Oaks, her eldest, is president of Brigham Young University. Merrill C. Oaks is an ophthalmologist in Provo. Evelyn Oaks Hammond, a graduate of BYU and returned missionary from France, is now a wife and mother.

Sister Oaks was the recipient of the Joseph F. Smith Family Living Award at the Brigham Young University commencement in 1975.

STELLA OAKS

"Thy Will Be Done"

To find one's own personal relationship with Heavenly Father, to never doubt that he guides the details of our lives, to be able in life's conflict to say, "Thy will be done," is the attaining of the ability to walk by faith. This ability is something that each soul must find in his own way through the creative living-out of any and all trying experiences that may come along. My proving ground came in learning to be obedient to a frightening command—that of accepting the imminent death of my husband after only eleven years of marriage and accepting the challenge of being a mother and woman alone in the world.

I had watched Lloyd become weaker and lose ground from day to day. This happened in spite of the blessings (which I interpreted as promises) that he should yet perform a great work upon the earth and that thousands would be given their sight through his skillful hands. How could he die when his fellow high councilors in the Twin Falls Stake, and later in the Denver Stake, had gathered about his bed in fasting, prayer, and administration, blessing him with recovery of health? An apostle of the Lord had blessed him to rise in health and continue his professional work and family responsibility. The spirit of peace was reassuring in the presence of these brethren of the priesthood. I felt that I must not let him die from any lack of faith on my part. Did his blessing not say that he had not chosen his profession alone—that God had imposed it upon him? Surely seven brief years of medical practice could not fulfill such an assignment.

But new complications continued to arise, and after reassuring myself with these thoughts, I would then be cast into utter despair and an even deeper gloom. I interpreted all this to mean that I was the one holding up the fulfillment of his blessings because I lacked faith. I censured myself and searched my soul. I learned to fast and pray on a level I had not previously known was possible. I am sure now that my determination and love kept him alive months longer than need have been.

One June night I knelt alone in prayer, utterly spent, wondering at that midnight hour how humble one had to be to receive an answer to one's pleading. It was just at that moment that I felt an envelopment of the spirit of peace, a profound assurance that God is over all and that it was his will that was in command and not mine. I could finally say, "Thy will be done," and feel the peace instead of guilt. I relaxed in my faith and discovered that I had a new trust in the Lord.

But even though this sweet peace enveloped me I still could not sleep, and once more I turned on the light. As I reached for the Doctrine and Covenants, it seemed to be actually propelled off the table into my hands; it fell open to a section where black velvet, raised letters indicated where I was to begin and end. I then experienced an expanded power of perception. In a flash I knew some specific things! I knew that the Lord was calling Lloyd to a great mission where all the promised blessings would be fulfilled in greater measure than I could at present perceive. I was given to know that the Lord loved me and that I would be made equal to my mission. I felt an encircling love that has sustained me ever since that great moment of change in my life. I have had continual hardships and challenges but always the sure knowledge that Jesus is the Christ, our Redeemer, and that he sustains us through the opposition that must arise in all things.

I am daily grateful for the degree of faith and trust I have in my Heavenly Father. When people have asked how I have managed to successfully rear my children, work in the Church, and hold responsible civic and professional positions, I can only reply that it is through day-by-day dependence on the Lord and by acknowledging his hand in all things.

———◆———

STELLA OAKS

"Promises Fulfilled"

We were living in Twin Falls, Idaho, at the time of my husband's death. I had the serious concern of my ability to meet the needs of our three children, Dallin, aged seven, Merrill, three and a half, and Evelyn, fourteen months. I wondered how I would even be able to drive the car 250 miles in the move back to Utah County. How would I be able to earn enough to educate the children as Lloyd and I had planned?

Then there was the problem of making the adjustment back to a career of teaching when all my dreams, expectations, and careful preparations were geared to the rearing of a large family and my role as a wife. I knew I could not perform my responsibilities alone, but my spirit was disciplined to covenant with the Lord. I would do all things he desired of me. This decision was also helped by the phrase my husband had uttered so many times during our family prayers: "We dedicate all our time, talents, and energies to Thy service." I felt sealed within this promise.

But it takes great spiritual effort to walk constantly by faith, and I had much learning to do as I was trying to meet the demands of daily survival and decision making. The words of my blessing came vividly to my consciousness: "Cry unto the Lord and he will hear thee and what seemeth a mountain shall become a molehill because of thy faith and integrity."

Several distinct blessings came to me at that very time of communion with the Lord. I was able to drive the car back to Utah with great ease; previously I had not driven farther than

Burley, some forty miles away. Contrary to my former needs, I was now able to feel completely invigorated after only five to six hours' sleep. My Father in heaven had also blessed me with three choice spirits to raise, and I discovered in them a strong sense of our family mission. They were equally dedicated to the goal of a happy, cooperative home. Another great blessing was the arrival of an unexpected insurance policy, which enabled me to pay off my husband's medical school expenses.

Before leaving to take up my new life and doubled parental responsibility, I sought a blessing from our stake patriarch, L.G. Kirkman, who promised me specific blessings. I was promised, depending on my faith, that my children would be able to have all the education they would desire. I was promised the strength to maintain a strong united home. I was also told that I would be able to make a personal contribution in both my profession and in my community. Let me explain the fascinating ways these promises have been fulfilled to the letter.

In his senior year at Brigham Young University, Dallin came home one day to tell me that he had been awarded the first University of Chicago Law School scholarship ever to be awarded to a BYU student. I was overjoyed and thought back to the blessing I had received fourteen years before. On another occasion the blessing was brought back to my mind when late one afternoon I arrived home from the school board office and found a letter addressed to my son Merrill. He opened it later in the evening and we were thrilled to discover that he had been granted a scholarship from the National Health Foundation, providing his fees for a full medical school education. He was accepted at five medical schools. I later discovered that this was their only scholarship awarded in Utah. As Evelyn was beginning college, she received the highly competitive Elks scholarship, providing her with books and tuition fees for the duration of her undergraduate degree. Later she was awarded a scholarship from the BYU College of Family Living, which enabled her to attend the Merrill Palmer College of Family Living in Detroit.

"If She Will Only Accept Her Mission"

I had many doubts when faced with rearing my three children alone, and at times I feared greatly as to how things would turn out. Would my children be well-adjusted, responsible, healthy adults? What would be the effects on them of not having a father to guide and teach them their roles and responsibilities? The worry was more in terms of probability than actuality, as I began to discover in little ways through different experiences with my children. Three incidents stand out as particularly good illustrations of how successful a woman can be rearing her children without the help of a husband, if she will only accept her mission, conquer her sense of loss, and maintain a wholesome cheerfulness and sense of security in the home and within herself.

The first happened when Dallin had graduated from high school at the age of seventeen, and I had given him permission to travel with a friend to Detroit to buy a new family car and drive it back to Utah. It was when I received a postcard from him thanking me for the trust I had placed in him that I was strengthened in my feeling that the Lord was pleased with our efforts as a family.

Later, when Merrill was fourteen, he came home from junior high school one afternoon and began talking to me as I prepared our evening meal. He told me about some of his school friends who used their parents' car without first asking permission. I became curious about Merrill's attitude toward this and asked him if he had ever felt inclined to take our car without my permission. "Of course not, Mother. You trust me too much. It wouldn't be any fun at all."

There were many times when I came home from the office, tired and not looking forward to the household duties that awaited me, to find that Evelyn, as a surprise, had prepared the evening meal, cleaned the house, and made cookies for her brothers. Already her thoughtful, selfless personality had begun to express itself in countless loving acts. Her homemaker's creativity was beginning to blossom also. She planned the remodeling of our kitchen. She has designed and made her own clothes since her days in junior high school. She was also a great companion. During the times she would put her hair up, we would relay the events of the day or I would read to her from such works as *The Lady of the Lake*.

The highlight of our week was Sunday. I cannot express the joy of walking to Sunday meetings with my children. Sunday saw us all together and at these times I was uplifted and reassured in my dual parental role because of the companionship and family unity we all felt. Often other family members would join us or we would be included in their gatherings. It was surprising to realize that without Lloyd we were able to feel such a complete and fulfilled family unit, and I can only attribute this to the Lord.

In addition to the many blessings that came to me through my children were those personal blessings and learning experiences of my own through involvement in professional and community responsibilities. Time and again I found myself a valued colleague on an all-male committee. I felt the warmth and acceptance of these men and discovered that women have much to offer in any and all positions of responsibility. To receive this confirmation of my effectiveness, and particularly of my femininity, was especially healing during the time that I was still struggling with the experience of losing Lloyd.

◄—►

STELLA OAKS

"My Hands Were Trembling"

I feel now to share some details of my greatest trial and learning experience I had after Lloyd's death. Having fortified myself intellectually and accepted my situation, I decided to go back to Columbia University to study for my master's degree. My dear parents were willing to take my children to their farm and care for them while I was away. Within six months I was on my way to graduate school. Although I was leaving everything and everyone familiar to me, I felt I could take anything for a period of six short months. But I found this to be wrong. As weeks went by and my heart began to ache more and more for my children and home, I studied harder and longer in an effort to cope.

One day as I was trying to write, I was aware my hands were trembling and that I could no longer recall the names of my children. I was also aware of how much weight I had lost. I began to sob and felt myself engulfed in a dark abyss from which I had not the power to raise myself. Though I was within three weeks of finishing the term, I could not do it. I was given incomplete grades and comforted by a counselor who said that in six or eight years I would get hold of myself and be able to return for completion. I was sent home with a psychiatric nurse, and because I had professional medical help within the family, I was allowed to be cared for by my loved ones, out on the farm where I could roam, work hard at physically strenuous tasks, and get well at my own rate.

It was a dark period and I remember that if I accidently glanced at big headlines in the newspaper, I would cry, for I was completely turned against any form of printed word, even letters from friends or family. The agony of those first weeks cannot be described to anyone, for I felt that I had lost my very self and my soul.

After about two months I could finally sleep from sheer physical exhaustion, and I began to feel a great loneliness for my children. It was at this time that I had a strong assurance of the love and approval of my husband. President Harold B. Lee once said that our loved ones are as near as we desire them to be and as we deserve and need them to be. I had this blessing. I have never been able to know why this experience befell me, but later on I would find myself repeating from Ephesians 3:13, "Wherefore I desire that ye faint not at my tribulations for you, which is your glory." But I do know that I have always had empathy and understanding of the deep personal struggles of those shaken souls who catch a glimpse of this abyss.

When I could lift myself to find the Lord, trust him, and

pick up my wounded self, I set up a daily schedule of service and work. I could then acknowledge the Lord's plan that all these experiences are for our good and benefit. When I remembered that the spirit had been placed in my body so that I might learn how to make it master in command of my body, one in purpose and accomplishment, I began to sense how to do this. I had my ideals and faith, but I had yet to learn how to recognize my physical and intellectual limitations and how to profitably seek to add spiritual solutions to my own determinations. I often think of the wise comment made by Rodney Turner in his book *Women and the Priesthood*, "Our ability to govern ourselves in righteousness is equal to the mastery which the spirit enjoys over its earthly tabernacle," but indeed this takes determination, trial and effort. Each of us must go through trials alone, learning attunement of body and spirit.

When I could exercise my will power (which is really spirit power), and the desire to rise up again and take hold of life's work and claim the many blessings that were mine, I began to make rapid progress. I returned to my children, to the work of settling the estate, to the renewal of peaceful Sabbaths, and to the dear rhythm of life. In one year I was teaching in high school and in two years I was able to return once again to New York, where, during summer terms, I completed requirements of a master's degree in guidance and personnel administration.

Although this experience settled me down to life's realities and responsibilities, it was years before I had the poise to tell or discuss these dark days. I feel I can say with President Spencer W. Kimball, "I have felt the refining change that comes only through suffering with those we love." Though these days are far behind me now, I would not be without the experience of growth and expansion that they brought. I learned to have compassion for others and to depend utterly on the Lord. "It is better that we pass through sorrow that we might know the good from evil" and align our lives that we might be fit to live with the Savior, and our loved ones, eternally.

KWANG KUN OK

"Little by Little, One Goes Far"

I was born of goodly parents as a first daughter in a small town near Pyund Yang, Korea, where my father used to be a medical doctor. God gave two daughters to our family consecutively, and my father made up his mind to make me a doctor to succeed his work. To my young mind I feel much pride in hearing my father saying that he would make me a doctor.

But when I was six, my father died of acute pneumonia, and my mother was left alone with the three children to look after (the other two children were two and four). Then my mother later remarried. . . . Under these unfavorable circumstances I was extremely lacking the necessary conditions for my better growing and learning.

But I enjoyed going to Sunday School, and I was very much interested in hearing the sermons of the adult members. In those days, some even said that there were not enough seats for little children and they did not want us to come to church. But some others complimented that I was doing well at church.

I prayed to our Father in heaven to help me to continue my study. I promised that I would look for the poor and afflicted, not for my own well-being and prosperity, if God would allow me to continue to study.

God opened the door for me.

With every hardship and poverty, I graduated from elementary and middle school. But I had to make a long-term plan for my higher education.

I always remembered the old sayings, "Discouragement is the thief of success" and "Little by little, one goes far," and the scriptures, ". . be not weary in well doing" and ". . serve the Lord with all thy mind." I never allowed myself to be stagnated or regressed. "Forward only" was my motto.

In 1941, I graduated from girls high school, but failed in entrance examination for the medical school. So I entered maternity nursing school in order to prepare for my qualification to be a doctor. I later entered college again.

In 1950, the Communists invaded my country and the Korean War broke out. Our country and people were once again driven into chaos. Many people lost their beloved families, and many children became orphans in a day.

In 1951, I graduated from college and was made a teacher for the refugees school. Those were the happy days in my life, and I tried to plant hope in the minds of our poor children.

In 1959, I went to the United States of America and entered the Baptist seminary. After finishing one semester I went to BYU and studied there for two years.

When I made up my mind to go to BYU, an American Presbyterian minister showed me a dictionary that explained the word *Mormon*. It said that Mormon was one of the religious sects that didn't believe in the Bible but in the Book of Mormon only, so the minister insisted that I not go to BYU. He said that if I stayed in California, he'd arrange for me a good job and school. But my mind already went to BYU. In two months at BYU, I knew that The Church of Jesus Christ of Latter-day Saints is not a false church as had been told by the minister.

But until I came back to Korea I did not decide which church I should be in. I couldn't easily give up my old faith and church. After one year's pondering and thinking I chose Mormonism and on June 23, 1962, I was baptized to become a Mormon.

After conversion I served as a Junior Sunday School coordinator, Relief Society visiting teacher, and Relief Society president in Seoul West Branch. I served as branch Relief Society president for seven years and district Relief Society president for two years, and I have served as mission Relief Society president for one and a half years.

In 1951 after graduation from college in Korea I had taught students for seven years. In 1965 I began to work as a mother of orphans. In 1969 I was forced into difficulties. If I continued to go to the Mormon Church, the board of directors of the orphanage, of which I was a principal, said that they would dismiss me; they insisted that I give up the church work. I couldn't agree with their suggestions, so I quit the orphanage with nine children who could sing very well. With those nine children I came to my little house, which I built in those years when I taught school.

At present there are thirty members in our "family," and our group is called Tender Apples. They are all students, attending primary, middle, and high school. One of my "daughters" graduated from college, and she is now preparing for a mission call.

In 1969 Brother Stan Bronson organized the Tender Apple Foundation and has supported us financially. Several times we have met difficult times, but I have tried to do my best to overcome them. We never thank enough Brother Bronson, the director of this foundation; Milton Thetcher, his assistant; and the other members who are our supporters. I think the only way to compensate for this is to watch over my "children" to grow up loving the Lord and make them lovely daughters of God.

◄——►

EIKA OLSEN

"You Always Have Five Minutes"

"**D**o you have five minutes?" The question struck a responsive chord. And although I didn't have time to talk to those missionaries, I remembered that a friend once said that "if you have any time for your fellowmen, you must have time to listen to those who tell others of their beliefs. You always have five minutes." So I invited them in.

Their message was interesting, and after their second visit a feeling began to grow inside me that maybe their words were true. However, my husband would have none of it. After I had visited with them four or five times, my husband became so angry that he threatened to leave me and the children if I didn't put an end to their visits.

We vacationed in Austria that summer, and I tried to forget about religion, but I had such mixed feelings that after we came home to Denmark I told my husband that I must earnestly pray to know whether or not the message of the missionaries was true. He replied, "That's a good idea, and when you have done that, we won't talk about it any more."

For three days I kept the Word of Wisdom and sought the Lord in prayer, but my prayers seemed empty words to me. Still, I persisted, and finally I found myself offering a sincere prayer with faith in Christ. I knew when I arose from my knees that if I didn't get an answer, I wouldn't pray any more. An hour later the doorbell rang. It was the missionaries.

When they walked into our living room, a strange feeling came over me. It started in my head and went completely through me, and I knew that my prayers had been answered. I went into the bedroom to thank the Lord and I laughed and cried and prayed, all at the same time.

When I returned to the living room, the elders told me they had been teaching a lady that day when they suddenly had nothing more to say to her. This had never happened to them before, but they made another appointment with her and left. On their way to the next appointment, they found themselves outside our apartment building, and our little boy ran up to them and asked if they were going to visit his mother. Since they had been rejected there before, they debated the matter, but one of them said the Spirit strongly impressed him to call. Ten days later, I was baptized.

There is a lovely conclusion to my story. At this time one of the General Authorities of the Church was visiting in Denmark and the missionaries took me to see him. He told me that if I would follow the counsel of Church leaders, it wouldn't be long before my husband was baptized. Surely he has made a mistake, I thought. My husband will never join the Church. That same evening my branch president asked me what I thought of the Church and I answered, "I have found so much love here." Then he said to me, "That same love you feel here you must take home to your husband."

I was a little angry. I loved my husband and thought such counsel unnecessary. But on the long drive home, I realized that I must speak kindly to my husband about the Church. My change of attitude made him curious, and when the children came home from church with sparkling eyes, he really began to investigate. Three months later my husband and our eight-year-old boy were baptized. It was truly one of the happiest days of my life.

Ensign, July 1974, p. 41.

ANN HARTLEY PARKER[*]

"The Shawl"

Arthur Parker was one of the four children of Robert and Ann Hartley Parker. While crossing the plains with the McArthur Handcart Company, Robert was stricken with fever and had to be placed in one of the wagons. This meant that Martha Alice had to leave her little brother to the care of other children and lend her child-strength to the heavy cart. What happened is told by Camilla Woodbury Judd:

One day, while going through the timberlands of Nebraska, Arthur became feverish and ill and, unnoticed by the other children, sat down to rest beside the trail. He was soon fast asleep. In the afternoon a sudden storm came up and the company hurried to make camp. Finding that Arthur was not with the children, they hurriedly organized a posse and went back to search for him. They returned with grim faces after two days' searching. The captain ordered the company to move on. Ann pleaded with him, but he set his jaw hard—the food was giving out and not another day could be lost.

Ann Parker pinned a bright shawl about the thin shoulders of her husband and sent him back alone on the trail to search again for their child. If he found him dead he was to wrap him in

[*]Ann Hartley Parker and her husband, Robert, were converts to the Church from England. In May 1856 they sailed to America. They were the parents of six children.

the shawl; if alive, the shawl would be a flag to signal her. Ann and her children took up their load and struggled on with the company, while Robert retraced the miles of forest trail, calling, searching, and praying for his helpless little son. At last he reached a mail and trading station. where he learned that his child had been cared for by a woodsman and his wife. He had been ill from exposure and fright. God had heard the prayers of his people.

Out on the trail each night Ann and her children kept watch, and when, on the third night, the rays of the setting sun caught the glimmer of a bright red shawl, the brave little mother sank in a pitiful heap in the sand. Completely exhausted, Ann slept for the first time in six long days and nights. God indeed was kind and merciful, and in the gladness of their hearts the Saints sang, "All is well. . . ."

Kate B. Carter, comp., *Treasures of Pioneer History* (Daughters of the Utah Pioneers), vol. 5, pp. 240-41.

Biographical Sketch

JAYNANN MORGAN PAYNE

Jaynann Morgan Payne was born and reared in Utah and was graduated from Brigham Young University with a major in English and a minor in Spanish and music. She is married to Dean W. Payne, a Provo, Utah, attorney, and they are the parents of twelve children, the last two being twin girls. Mrs. Payne states, "It may not be cheaper by the dozen, but it certainly is more fun!"

In 1967, Sister Payne became Mrs. Utah after a friend entered her name in the statewide contest. She went to San Diego with her husband to participate in the Mrs. America pageant and, after winning the entertainment events for adults, teens, and children, and placing high in many other events, she was named the second runner-up to Mrs. America of 1967-68. She gives the credit for her honor to her husband because he has always treated her "like a queen." She has said, "Happiness is being second runner-up to Mrs. America when you have a dozen children who need you at home and who are the real jewels in the only crown I want."

Sister Payne has taught in Sunday School, Relief Society, and MIA since the age of sixteen and has also served as president of a ward MIA. Since 1967 she has given many lectures to church and civic organizations, family life meetings, and youth conferences. She has been awarded a special commendation of merit by the city of Provo for her family, community, and church service. She is lecturer and special instructor for BYU and has participated in many television and radio programs for youth and parents.

She is the author of several books, including *The Art of Accomplishment* and *Beauty for Keeps,* and she co-authored *The Joy of Being a Woman* with many other outstanding LDS women.

JAYNANN MORGAN PAYNE

"I Enjoy Being a Girl"

I enjoy being a girl because girls can become mothers. You will never have a greater opportunity to put real beauty into practice, to do good to those that hurt you, or to be forgiving than you will as a mother.

One of the most provocative experiences I had at the Mrs. America Pageant happened because we had the largest family. We only had ten children then, but everyone knew it. Mrs. Connecticut was second with nine children, and people said to both of us, "You must be either Mormon or Catholic." She was Catholic and I was Mormon. We became great friends. People were always asking me, *sotto voce,* "What are you, a one-woman world population explosion?" But the barb that left me speechless and nonplussed was from a crusty, bass-voiced woman reporter who said, "You've got your nerve, bringing ten children into this lousy world of hate, war, death, and destruction!" I couldn't think of one word to utter.

But since then, like Charlie Brown's Snoopy, who sits on top of his doghouse thinking up perfect replies, I have finally come up with the perfect answer. Recently, in doing some genealogy, I noticed that many of my great-grandparents raised only about half of their ten to fifteen children because disease wiped out the other half. My husband's great-uncle lost four of his six children during a diphtheria epidemic while he was on a mission. He had four darling babies when he left and none when he returned. He and his wife had to begin all over again.

I do wish that that reporter would repeat her statement to me again someday, because now I am prepared and I would let her have it with both barrels. I'd say, "Nonsense, my dear, there has never been a better time in the world to have a dozen children. See, we have even had twins since last we met. A child has never had a better chance to grow to healthy adulthood, and to gain an education, and to live a productive life. It's just no time to raise sissies. Good mothers are not born—they are made—and it is a nitty-gritty process. There should be hopes and dreams verbalized, confidences shared, commitment encouraged, the windows of heaven opened, ears listening to souls, weaknesses worked on together, and above all, love—God-like, unconditional, and eternal, flowing and vitalizing and regenerating every member."

"Beauty for Keeps," *Speeches of the Year*, Brigham Young University, February 10, 1970, pp. 10-11.

◄—►—►

JAYNANN MORGAN PAYNE

"He Will Always Be in the Audience"

Have you ever wondered what your children will look like? How they will sound? What they will say?

When I was in college, the nesting instinct seized me and I began a scrapbook of poetry about children and pictures of babies and children—interesting things I wanted to keep. One day a picture of the most beautiful little girl I had ever seen caught my eye. Her reddish-brown curls glinted around mischievous blue eyes. Her delight in holding a downy baby chick to her cheek showed in her dimpled hands and cheeks. "Oh, if only my children would someday be that pretty," I thought.

Do you know that I still have that picture? Guess whose wildest dreams came true! My children are even more beautiful than I ever expected, and yours will be too. It will be a miracle. You will look into your baby's face, and the breathtaking wonder of the universe, a testimony of God, will be in your baby's face. It is the choicest experience a woman can have.

A man cannot experience birth except vicariously. He can sit and hold your hand, he can give you encouragement and be a strong, powerful influence for you to lean on, but he will always be in the audience and not on stage. You will never be closer to your Father in heaven than when you give birth to your miracle child, the child that can lead you back into your Father's presence.

"Beauty for Keeps," p. 11.

<hr>

JAYNANN MORGAN PAYNE

"If Only I Had Known Five Minutes Before"

We will never forget that sweet young girl of sixteen who came to live with us one summer for the remaining months of her unwed pregnancy. My husband is an attorney and was handling the adoption of her baby. She hadn't wanted to marry the boy who was the father of her unborn child. She had been beguiled and had partaken of the bitter fruit.

In September she gave birth to a beautiful little boy, and the day she was to leave the hospital, Dean and I had to go to Salt Lake City. We stopped at the hospital long enough to meet the couple who were adopting the baby. Under hospital rules, this young mother, sixteen years old, had to take her beautiful nine-pound boy from the arms of the nurse and hand him over to my husband, who then stepped outside the room and gave the baby to the adopting parents. It tore me apart to watch her and to see that young couple leave with her baby.

She said to me, "Sister Payne, he lied to me when he said nobody would get hurt, and that because we loved each other, anything we did was alright. He didn't really love me. That is why I didn't marry him, because he wasn't worthy to be the father of my little boy. It's all a great big lie, and I don't want to live a lie!

"Oh, if only I had known five minutes before I was immoral how I would feel five minutes after I gave my baby away!"

For this girl not to have thought ahead about the consequences of her actions and not to have realized that lust is the mere image of love is indeed heartbreaking. It is so important to keep in tune, keep in touch, to receive the Spirit each and every day. We never know what is going to happen; and if we make the commitment in our private rooms, by the side of our beds, to our Father in heaven, of what we want to be in life—what we will do and what we won't do—and then ask for his help in keeping our commitments, he will help us in public and private.

"Beauty For Keeps," p. 8.

◀—▶

JAYNANN MORGAN PAYNE

"Someday I May Be a Real Queen"

As the announcer called out the name of the third runner-up in the Mrs. America competition, only three of us were left on that big, bright, lonely stage. My knees got rather wobbly and words of the missionary song ran through my mind: I'll go where you want me to go, dear Lord, but please let it be home to my husband and family! I felt strongly that to be gone from my husband and family for most of a year was wrong. Almost immediately my prayer was answered and my husband, Dean, came rushing out on stage as they called out: "Mrs. Utah, second runner-up!" He grabbed me, gave me the bouquet of roses, and we hugged each other and laughed and kissed each other. Everyone offstage thought we had cracked up from the strain. They couldn't believe we were so happy.

Then the former Mrs. America brought a beautiful diamond crown and a red velvet robe with a white ermine collar, placed them on Mrs. Kansas, and crowned her Mrs. America. Mrs. Kansas was a perfect Mrs. America because she only had two children, both in school, her mother lived near enough to watch her children while their mother was away, and her husband could arrange his work to travel with her some of the time. Marlene, the new Mrs. America, was a dark-haired, vivacious woman, with many talents—a beautiful American homemaker.

But as I stood there on stage watching the coronation, the most significant experience of those ten wonderful days occurred. These thoughts came to me as I watched Mrs. America crowned:

"She is a queen for only a very short year. That crown and robe will be given to someone else next year. How typical of the honors of men! But I am the most fortunate and blessed of all these fifty best homemakers in the country. I am the only one who has had the privilege of going through the temple and of wearing the robes of a real queen. If I will get on the ball and really work, someday I may be a *real* queen, not just for a day, a year, or thirty years, but for time and all eternity. I also have twelve beautiful children who are genuine jewels in an eternal crown, and a prince of a husband who magnifies the priesthood of God. What greater honor and joy is there in all the world than to be a queen and handmaiden in the kingdom of the Lord and Savior, Jesus Christ?"

"Beauty for Keeps," pp. 18-20.

ELECTA PECK

"She Arose, Dressed Herself . . ."

During the third conference of the Saints, in 1831, the Saints were told to go to Kirtland, Ohio. As one particular group started on its way, Brother Newel Knight relates that he was subpoenaed as a witness and had to return to his home town in New York. The company decided to wait for him.

Brother Knight continues:

"After I left, my aunt, Electa Peck, fell and broke her shoulder in a most shocking manner; a surgeon was called upon to relieve her sufferings, which were very great. My aunt dreamed that I returned and laid my hands upon her, prayed for her, and she was made whole and pursued her journey with the company. She related this dream to the surgeon, who replied, 'If you are able to travel in many weeks, it will be a miracle, and I will be a Mormon, too.'

"I arrived at the place where the company had stopped, late in the evening; but on learning of the accident, I went to see my aunt, and immediately upon entering the room, she said, 'O, Brother Newel, if you will lay your hands upon me, I shall be well and able to go on the journey with you.' I stepped up to the bed and, in the name of the Lord Jesus Christ, rebuked the pain with which she was suffering and commanded her to be made whole; and it was done, for the next morning, she arose, dressed herself, and pursued the journey with us to Kirtland."

Newell Knight, "Scraps of Biography," Juvenile Instructor Office, 1883, p. 19.

SISTER PERKINS

"Contrary to the Order of God"

We attended the sick both night and day and our success was marvelous, because the Lord blessed the medicine we used, it being such as he had ordained for the benefit of his Saints, using no poison, nor bleeding, nor starving of our patients.

At one time there was so much sickness it was five days and nights that I never entered my own door. We worked hard against the power of death, which fooled me out of two patients through my ignorance.

Hyrum Perkins and his wife were very sick when I first visited them. I attended them with a good prospect of their recovery. They got quite smart. I visited them one morning as usual, and they were so smart they thought they were going to get well. The woman said to me, "I ain't going to take any more medicine." "Why?" said I. "Because I had a vision last night," said she, "and was told that we both will get well now without the medicine." I believed it as well as they did and left off, and they both died in a short time.

I told Brother Richards the circumstances and he gave me a very brotherly rebuke and said, "Don't you ever believe in the visions or revelations of a woman to govern her husband. It is contrary to the order of God." I have ever since been cautious on that subject. A woman may counsel her husband but not control him.

Kate B. Carter, comp., *Our Pioneer Heritage* (Daughters of the Utah Pioneers, 1959), vol. 2, p. 85.

JANE SNYDER RICHARDS

"One Potato for the Sick Child"

On June 10, 1846, Franklin D.
Richards wrote:

"I accepted the offer of two yoke of oxen, a wagon, a jack
screw, a chain and a whip, the whole valued at not to exceed one
hundred and twenty-five dollars, in exchange for a two-story
brick house and an acre of ground, which my neighbors a year
ago considered worth five hundred dollars. About sunset we bade
adieu to our little home in Nauvoo."

After arriving in Sugar Creek, on July 3 he committed his
loved ones to the protecting care of Divine Providence and
turned his face sadly, yet resolutely, toward the east, without
money and with scant clothing, to make his way across the
continent and ocean into a strange land to fulfill a mission he was
called to prior to the death of Joseph Smith.

Jane Snyder Richards started out for the West without her
husband, and twenty days after leaving Sugar Creek, she gave
birth to her second child, a son whom she named Isaac; but the
babe had barely opened its eyes upon this world when it was
summoned to the spirit land. The picture of this homeless pil-
grim mother, lying helpless in her wagon on the broad, lonely
prairie, her dead babe on her breast and her husband a thousand
miles away, was pitiful enough to melt a heart of stone.

At this time her only remaining child, Wealthy, not yet three years old, was lying sick, having been stricken by disease shortly after they left Sugar Creek. As they approached the Missouri River she gradually grew weaker and weaker. She had scarcely eaten anything for a month or more. She was very fond of potatoes, and one day, while passing a farm in the midst of a fine field of these vegetables, hearing them mentioned, she asked for one. Jane Snyder Richards's mother went to the house to ask if they could have one potato for the sick child. "I wouldn't sell or give one of you Mormons a potato to save your life," was the woman's brutal reply. She had even set her dog upon Sister Snyder when she saw her approaching.

Wealthy died on the 14th of September and was buried at Cutler's Park, a little west of the Missouri River. The first night Brother Richards arrived in Liverpool he wrote, "Today my little daughter, Wealthy, if she lives, is three years old. May her life and health be precious in thy sight, O Lord."

Franklin L. West, *Life of Franklin D. Richards* (Deseret News Press, 1924), pp. 68-71.

ANNA-LIISA RINNE*

"If You Love Him, Why Not Serve Him?"

In 1959 I was living in Helsinki, Finland, with my four children and working toward a specialty in pediatrics. Although I was a doctor, we had little money, and my hours were long and strenuous. Having lost my sweetheart in World War II, and because of a later unfortunate marriage, I had an unhappy attitude toward life, and religion brought me no comfort. My only real joys were my wonderful children.

Then one day two young men called at my door and said they were representing The Church of Jesus Christ of Latter-day Saints. I would have turned them away, but that long, strange name sparked something in my memory. Ten years earlier I had read an article in a magazine about a man from America who claimed to be an apostle. I like what this man, Ezra Taft Benson, had said about the doctrines of his church. I thought then that this might be the true church, if there was one. But too busy to think more about it, I had brushed all such thoughts from my mind. Now two of its representatives were standing at my door.

As the missionaries testified of the First Vision and of the

*Anna-Liisa Rinne, a pediatrician, studied medicine at the University of Helsinki and was graduated in 1947. In January 1975 she was called as a health missionary for the Church and is serving in Western Samoa. She is the mother of two sons, one of whom has completed a mission, and two daughters.

Lord's reply to young Joseph that there was not a true church on earth, amazingly I believed them. I even accepted the story of Lehi and bought a Book of Mormon.

It was good to hear of the plan of salvation and the purpose of life. But when they suggested baptism, I replied with an emphatic "No!" I did not want to become a member of any religious group. I wanted to keep my freedom. Besides, I was afraid of what my neighbors would think. "Thank you," I told them. "Now that I know what I want to know, you need not come back anymore." And they didn't.

But in my heart there was no peace. On Sunday I slipped into a Latter-day Saint meeting. The spirit overwhelmed me, and a witness came to my soul. I knew the gospel was true and that I must join this church.

Strangely enough, I was not happy about it. I felt trapped and I was still afraid my neighbors would turn against me. So I decided not to tell them; but on the day of our baptism my young son, who had just turned eight, went out and happily told all the neighbors that now we were Mormons. I had to face it. They laughed at me at first, but as weeks went by the hurt subsided and I was not afraid. A new joy filled my heart. I had found the true church. I could read and learn more and more. I could begin to know my Redeemer.

Perhaps my most faith-promoting experience was in helping to build our chapel in Kuopio in the early 1960s. Our small branch consisted of three elders and about eighty women. Constructing the meetinghouse was difficult, but with the help of some building missionaries and the guidance of our project supervisor, we saw it completed. I was very busy with my profession at the time, being the only pediatrician in the city, but I sincerely wanted to help on the building.

Then, curiously, a pediatrician came to our hospital and I was able to have him cover some of my calls. (He left Kuopio soon after the chapel was completed.)

Laboring on the building was often hard and the weather sometimes got very cold. The temperature often dropped to 20 degrees below zero, numbing my hands until I could hardly hold the hammer and nails. Then I would repeat the words of a song to motivate me and give rhythm to my hammering: "If you love Him, why not serve Him?" It consisted of four beats—four hits with my hammer. I have adopted this for my motto.

Now I am privileged to serve as supervisor of the Finland Mission Relief Society, and a dream of many years was fulfilled last year when I visited Utah and got to know some dedicated people there. Since 1961 I have participated in semiannual excursions to the Swiss Temple and have completed 157 endowments. My two daughters have married in the temple, and one of my sons has completed a mission.

Ensign, July 1974, p. 44.

MAVA McAFFEE RUSSON*

"A Beautiful Blessing"

I came from a family that loved the great outdoors. Boating and fishing were just part of our lives.

I have a brother Boyd, who, three weeks after he married and was graduated from BYU, completely and totally collapsed with a rare muscle disease called myasthenia-gravis. Little was known of the disease at that time. He was taken to the Mayo Clinic in Rochester, Minnesota, for three months of medical treatment. The doctors gave him little hope to live.

A few months later my father's vacation time came, and Dad and Mother both felt it would be good for Boyd if we took him with us on a little vacation to Bear Lake, Idaho.

On August 1, 1941, Dad asked Mother and me if we would like to pack a lunch and go across the lake for a day of fishing with him. We made Boyd comfortable at camp, and neighbors agreed to look in on him, since he didn't feel well enough to go with us. Mother and I packed a lunch and off the three of us went and spent a great day together. We were returning at about six P.M. when a terrible, violent windstorm came up. Our

---

*Mava McAffee Russon lived in Salt Lake City and later moved to Lehi, Utah, where she met Dale Russon. They were married in the Salt Lake Temple and are the parents of four children. They are now serving as missionaries, as President Russon presides over the California Oakland Mission.

fourteen-foot boat was capsized and we were thrown into the water. We had our life preservers, and we battled the storm and waves for what seemed like an eternity. The waves were the largest I had ever seen. A powerful wave would come down on top of us and knock us away from the boat; just as we would make our way back to the overturned boat, another big wave would come down on top of us and knock us away again. We battled like this until the storm finally subsided. Mother did not make it back to the overturned boat, and she drowned. It was getting dark and cold and we could not find her body.

Dad and I knew that Boyd would send someone looking for us when we didn't return. Oh, how earnestly we prayed that long, cold night that we would be saved. At age sixteen, I had an unusual amount of faith in my Father in heaven and felt that we would be rescued.

During that long, cold night, our overturned boat began to sink from the weight of the two motors; the only part of the boat that didn't sink was about sixteen inches of the bow, and this was all we had to hold on to. The only parts of our bodies that were out of the water were our heads.

Boyd was alarmed when we didn't return, and a search party began looking for us at daybreak. After twenty-one hours in the water and one-half hour before rescuers found our boat, my father also drowned. I was still clinging to the overturned boat, suffering from shock and exposure. Mother's body was found floating a short distance away.

Boyd was waiting on the pier for us. When he saw me he literally picked me up and carried me to the car and drove to the house trailer where we were staying. (Boyd received strength from our Heavenly Father when needed; up to this point he had hardly been able to stand up or feed himself because of his sickness.)

My other brother, Don, and friends, neighbors, and relatives came from Salt Lake City to see if they could help in any way. Don headed the search party for Dad's body. Every day for twenty-eight days they dragged the lake until they finally found his body.

During those days our house trailer was always filled with people. One day a man dressed in white came in while I was lying in bed, placed his hands upon my head, and gave me a beautiful blessing. I will never forget what he said to me: "If you will

216

live the gospel the way that you should, the whys and wherefores of this accident will be made known unto you." No one saw him come in and no one saw him leave, but I know he was there and I will never forget what he said to me.

After the accident we were forced to sell our family home and move to another community. I became very bitter toward the Church and felt that if I had a Heavenly Father, he would have answered my prayers. Then I met Dale Russon, and through his love and understanding I was brought back into the Church. A few years later we were married in the Salt Lake Temple, and we are now the parents of four children.

Today I can honestly say that I know our accident was meant to be. Even though I didn't know it at the time, I now know that my prayers were being answered. I know that my life was spared because my Heavenly Father wanted me to be a mother in Israel and rear a family. I also know that my dad lived through that night on Bear Lake to comfort me and give me encouragement to hang on to the boat until I was rescued.

I know also that had it not been for the accident I would never have met my husband. And had it not been for Boyd's illness, he also might have drowned that day.

I am grateful for the reassurance I have that our Heavenly Father does not always answer our prayers in the way we think he should, but that he does answer them in a manner that is best for us. He has blessed me continually. I have a testimony of the gospel, and I love it with all my heart.

JEANETTE C. RYDER*

"Just for a Moment"

Today, after we had finished dinner, my eleven-year-old daughter said, "Come on, Mother, get your sweater."

"Where are we going?" I asked.

"Come on, get your sweater," she said, divulging nothing.

So, sweaters on, out the door we went. I followed her through the dead grass down to the river that runs past our place. She took me along the river's edge, then up among the willows and brush that grow on the shore.

"Can you make it?" she asked.

"I can go anywhere you can," I laughingly answered.

"Oh, I don't know," she joked back.

I followed her through the willows and brush, ducking under limbs, stepping over sticks, scratching my legs sometimes. We explored the river bank thoroughly. And she showed me her secret play spots. Then we raced back along the river's edge, laughing as she beat me to a group of big lava rocks. On across a fence, and among some trees, holding hands, we kicked through the autumn leaves that had fallen. Then we headed back for the house.

°Jeanette C. Ryder, a realtor in Idaho Falls, Idaho, is married to Lloyd Ryder and has four children and six grandchildren. A native of Rigby, Idaho, she has taught in the auxiliaries of the Church.

218

For awhile, out in the crisp autumn air, I had recaptured my youth. Such a bond my daughter and I felt as we walked hand in hand! I thought to myself, You need me because I am your mother. But I, too, need you. It takes such a little bit of love and companionship to make us feel close to one another.

Then I realized that in this busy world we must take time out to enjoy the small but beautiful things of the world with our children if we are to cement our relationships and our understandings. Just a few moments in their world means all the world to both of us.

Relief Society Magazine, May 1965, p. 384.

Biographical Sketch

ANNE KIRSTINE SMOOT

Anne Kirstine Morrison Smoot was born in Onsu, Norway, December 19, 1833. She heard the gospel for the first time in 1852, and she and her brother, Nels, were baptized on April 27, 1853. She left Norway in 1854 and went to Liverpool, England.

In January 1855, with a group of Saints, she set sail for America aboard the *James Nesmitt*. Elder O. P. Hansen had charge of the company of Saints, which consisted of 600 persons from Norway, Sweden, Denmark, Germany, and Ireland. She arrived in Salt Lake City in September of that year.

Anne married Bishop A. O. Smoot on February 17, 1856, in a ceremony performed by President Brigham Young. She was the mother of three sons and four daughters. One of her sons, Reed Smoot, was a member of the Council of the Twelve and a United States Senator.

Sister Smoot served as president of the Utah Stake Primary in Provo. She died January 20, 1894.

ANNE KIRSTINE SMOOT

"A Few Words from Your Daughter Kirstine"

As told by Elder Reed Smoot

Together with Brother John A. Widtsoe, I had the privilege of visiting Europe during the months of July and August. While thus upon a special mission, and with the assistance of Brother Widtsoe, I had the privilege of visiting the Scandinavian countries. I took the time to go there primarily to visit my mother's old home. While a young man I used to say to Mother, "Someday we will go back to the old home." I left it too late, as so many things are put off until it is too late, for my mother died when she was sixty years old. But I had made up my mind that sooner or later I would go to the old home and see some of my relatives there.

I haven't the time to express the feelings I had when I stood upon the very spot where she was born, and when I saw the old door that she had opened perhaps hundreds and hundreds of times, when I looked upon the spring back of the house, which I had heard her speak of when I was a boy, and when I stood under the shade of that wonderful tree her mother had planted and which she used to tell me about. As I saw conditions surrounding that homestead, I thanked God from the bottom of my heart that the gospel of Jesus Christ reached my mother, and that she knew it was true, when she was but a girl. All opposition and all persecution on the part of her father and her mother and her loved ones never had one iota of influence upon her testimony that God lives and that Jesus is the Christ.

My cousins brought to me the old family Bible, and as I opened it, I saw a writing and at the bottom of the last page of it the name "Anna Kirstine Maurits-datter." I could not read the writing, but I asked Brother Widtsoe to copy it as quickly as possible, then tell me what was in it. I desired to have it translated word for word. It was a message to her parents written on the day that she left home—the day she was driven from home by a loving father and mother who thought that she would not be gone very long, but that she would soon return and ask forgiveness and deny that she knew that God lives and that Jesus is the Christ. She was only a girl then, but I am going to quote that letter because it gives forth the spirit that makes women such as she. It is filled full of the spirit of our fathers and mothers who were willing to sacrifice all in this world for the gospel's sake; aye, it is the spirit of a missionary, teaching the gospel of Jesus Christ. This was written in her own handwriting, and it was the last farewell of a girl who loved her country, who loved her father and mother, and who loved her home, but who loved the gospel of Jesus Christ more:

"A few words from your daughter Kirstine, Dear, my parents: Pray God for courage to accept this great truth contained in this book and now restored, so that rejected knowledge may not be a testimony against you on God's great day to come. I pray God that on that great day we may be able to gather together in joy and happiness, and that we may then be crowned to God's glory, and that he may say to us all: 'Come now, my faithful children, you shall be rewarded for your labors.' This matter, and my desire that you may know the truth and accept it, have made me shed in secret many burning tears, and they have been increased when I have thought of the ungodliness of mankind. The years are speeding on, the day is approaching when all must listen to the Shepherd and render obedience to his will, or receive punishment. The great King is coming to reign and to rule. Sin and evil will be banished. May God grant that you may be among the worthy ones. My heart grows tender when I think of these things. God give that all mankind may repent. I shall pray to my Heavenly Father that all who read these lines may comprehend the true purpose of his holy book, and may lay down the burden of sin. That which I have written is for all who may read these lines. I pray God to lead you into eternal life.

Kirstine Maurits-datter,
Drammen, Sept. 1, 1854

I am not ashamed of the gospel of Jesus Christ; I am not ashamed of the testimony of the mother that gave me birth. I care not where I go upon the face of the earth, whether it be with kings, potentates, or any class of people in the world; I want them all to know that I am a member of The Church of Jesus Christ of Latter-day Saints.

Conference Report, October 1923, pp. 76-77.

◄——►

ANNE KIRSTINE SMOOT

"You'll Live to See the Fulfillment"

When Senator Reed Smoot was a small boy, Brigham Young came to Provo and, at a conference meeting, said that the day would come when the human voice would be heard from New York to San Francisco.

Reed's mother had taken him to this meeting, and on the way home he said (referring to what President Brigham Young had said), "Now that's a big lie. That's absolutely impossible. It couldn't be." His mother, who was a woman of very great faith, told her son, "Yes, you'll live to see the fulfillment of what the President has said today." But he did not believe it.

Time went by, and while he was in the United States Senate, a broadcasting system was built so one could speak from New York City to San Francisco. One of his colleagues in the Senate had charge of this enterprise, and when it was completed and they were to celebrate the event, he invited Senator Smoot to come to New York City and be the first man to speak over the completed network, which he did, and his voice was heard clearly and distinctly across the continent.

Thus he lived to literally fulfill the promise by President Brigham Young in Provo years before.

Bryant S. Hinckley, *The Faith of Our Pioneer Fathers* (Deseret Book Co., 1956), p. 207.

BETTY G. SPENCER*

"The Neighbor Plate"

The well-worn, deep metal pie plate didn't look like anything valuable as it lay neglected in a kitchen drawer. An outsider would have quickly discarded it as something of little value, but to our family, gathered to prepare the house for new occupants, it represented a cherished characteristic of a friendly, vivacious grandmother.

The pie plate was what we called Grandmother's Neighbor Plate, and it was one of her most often used kitchen utensils.

Grandmother always seemed to make a little extra whenever she prepared a special treat for her family. Somehow, the extra was placed in the pie plate and carried to an appreciative friend or neighbor. When sickness, trouble, or death visited a neighborhood home, the pie plate inevitably was carried to the kitchen door, and the sorrowing family members were cheered by the delectable contents.

Grandmother, an excellent cook, was locally famous for her flaky pie crusts, mouthwatering fruitcakes, and feathery light hot rolls.

*Betty G. Spencer and her husband, Ralph, reside in American Fork, Utah, and are the parents of four children. Sister Spencer has had hundreds of magazine articles published and has won thirteen national writing awards. She is currently teaching in the Relief Society.

The Neighbor Plate helped Grandmother get acquainted with a newcomer, too. Moving day was sure to find her running over with a "little something" to help out with the first meal in the new home. We soon noticed that the Neighbor Plate was an important link in the close, warm friendships that grew along her street.

Frequently the plate was returned heaped with apples, berries, pieces of newly baked cake, or other special treats from grateful hearts. Gratitude delighted Grandmother, but those few neighbors who felt duty-bound to return the favor were a genuine disappointment. Grandmother felt that her offering should be savored, enjoyed—even appreciated—but not necessarily paid back.

Grandmother is gone now, but the philosophical values she implanted in our hearts are still with us.

Her daughters have remained in the same friendly mountain valley where they grew to womanhood, but the grandchildren have settled across the country from Florida to California. Our homes are as varied as we are, but each of us has an important piece of kitchen equipment. We would never think of keeping house without a Neighbor Plate.

Our Grandmother's philosophy of giving is as appropriate today as it was fifty years ago. What we give is not really too important. It may be lemon meringue pie in Florida or Hungarian goulash in California. Whatever else we may add, love and friendliness are the most important ingredients that are ever offered on a Neighbor Plate!

Relief Society Magazine, July 1965, p. 515.

CELESTIA J. TAYLOR[*]

"Grandma Nash"

In some ways, in the memories of my very early childhood, my Grandmother Nash—"Grandma" always to me—stands out even more vividly than does my mother. I can explain this perhaps best by saying that, because Mother was always there to be with and to come home to, I must have just taken her for granted, though I know now that without her through my life, I would have been lost.

I can hardly think of Grandma Nash without thinking of her home, which she loved so dearly. It was a brick structure of typical Victorian style, three stories high and comprising sixteen rooms, all furnished richly and completely with every comfort and luxury that was available at that time. How I loved that house of Grandma's! I knew every corner of it more intimately than I knew our own Alpine home.

Grandma was an immaculate housekeeper; there was order not only in every room in her house, but also on every shelf and in every drawer. It seems to me now, as I look back in nostalgic remembrance, that her home was a haven of perfection and

*Celestia J. Taylor and her husband, Lynn Dixon Taylor, are the parents of five children. A worker in the Provo Temple, she was on the English faculty at Brigham Young University for eighteen years and a member of the Relief Society general board twelve years.

228

peace. This, I know, is partly a romantic projection growing out of my childhood impressions, but nevertheless it is a very real one to me.

Something I can never forget was her sitting room just off her bedroom, where she did her handiwork. A glimpse into the drawers of her cabinets revealed rows and rows of variegated assortments of thread, embroidery floss, and yarn, all arranged in graduated color schemes from the palest tints to the deepest hues. To me, as a child, they were a fascinating sight. And her needlework was something to see. Her beautiful handmade quilts, rugs, and afghans; her exquisite hand embroidery; her peerless knitting and crocheting; her intricate patterns of featherstitching and piecework; her hand-loomed carpets and fabrics—all these and more testified of her talent as an artist in these skills.

Although Grandma was far more than domestic in her tastes and inclinations, in her kitchen she was perfection itself. I can still see her drawing from the oven a batch of fragrant bread or a pan of yeast biscuits, high and incredibly light; or see her rolling out the dough for her pies, which, except for those of my mother baked from the same recipe and method, have never been equaled in my experience. Her wonderful breads, pies, and cakes often found their way into the homes of her neighbors and friends in need. Hardly a day went by that did not see her taking something to someone.

I never saw her at work in her kitchen when she was not singing; in fact, I can hardly think of her without hearing her singing. Sometimes a note of sadness emanated from her songs, but whatever her mood, she expressed it in some kind of singing. Sometimes she merely hummed, but always I remember her with music in her heart. She knew from memory and dearly loved all the favorite Church hymns, and it was from hearing her sing them that I learned most of them myself. Her voice had a low, vibrant quality that had a penetrating effect upon my senses. Whenever I heard the words of King Lear in Shakespeare's great tragedy, "Her voice was ever soft, gentle, and low, an excellent thing in woman," I always think of my Grandmother Nash.

I think it must have been her gift of song that lent a buoyancy to her spirit to lift it up in spite of sorrows that could easily have destroyed a less indomitable character. Not from her did I hear the story of the loss of five beautiful children—four daughters and one son—within the space of six months, from diphtheria. These and many other trials seemed to have made her stronger in the bearing of them. There was never any wavering in her faith. She possessed a strong, personal testimony that kept her close to the Church and true to its principles as long as she lived.

Relief Society Magazine, May 1966, pp. 324-26.

EDITH M. THEAKER

"How Thankful We Are for All Our Blessings"

It was snowing heavily on the last Friday in January 1956, and I was feeling rather weary. Owing to severe heart trouble, I had, for a long time, been unable to exert my energy. My thoughts drifted back over eighteen years of happy marriage, how God had guided and helped George and me all our lives. But I was wondering, too. I was wondering why George had been born blind, why I had never been able to manage even a year without a doctor's care, and why our three children had lived only a short time. I quietly asked God, if it was his will, to help me understand these things.

A knock at the door roused me. When with difficulty I opened it, I saw two young ladies standing there. As I could not stand, I invited them in. They introduced themselves as Sister Butler and Sister Jones, explaining they were missionaries. After an enjoyable discussion about the gospel, they left me a copy of the Book of Mormon to read and arranged to call again the next Friday morning. Before they returned I read it through and told George about it.

As the weeks passed I realized that the message contained in this book was the answer to my prayers. Gradually I began to move about the house; and, by summer, the doctor said I could try going on a bus. The sisters—Sister Butler had been replaced

231

by Sister Jolly—took me out and we had lunch in town. We thanked our Father in heaven joyfully. Soon they took me to church and then to Relief Society.

My heart thrilled on the day of my baptism. George had agreed that I might go ahead, that he might follow later when he was more prepared. Because of an accident, I had been paralyzed since three years before our marriage. I had never been able to stand in water above my knees, and because my foot was not quite straight I could not walk without shoes or without a stick. The district and branch presidents asked me about this, and I could only reply that "Jesus did not ask people if they had any handicap. He just asked them to be baptized."

It was wonderful! The sisters helped me to the font, I left my shoes at the edge, and with help I entered the water. An awful blackness seized me as I went deeper, and in my heart I cried to God for help. And then everything cleared. I was baptized and walked out of the font and across the outer room without shoes or stick, just leaning on Sister Wilkinson's arm. There was joy in my heart!

I gradually improved. On April 13, 1957, George was baptized also, and our joy was complete. We were able to attend each auxiliary meeting and were called to work in the auxiliaries. And again our Heavenly Father blessed us.

How thankful we are for all our blessings! Not only are we thankful for bodily strength to do God's work, but also for spiritual strength to have hope and understanding. Now we understand why our son and two daughters had to leave us so soon and marvel to think that we were found worthy enough to give them earthly bodies so that they could once again dwell with God. We understand, through learning about the preexistence and resurrection, that God had his own reasons for George's blindness. Truly has God opened the windows of heaven and poured out upon us many blessings.

Millennial Star, vol. 120 (1958), pp. 109-10.

LUCILE TOURNEAR

"My Guiding Light"

My mother was so quiet and unassuming that many of her closest neighbors never really learned to know her; yet she was truly a friend to the friendless and a comfort to the lonely-hearted.

My early childhood would have been desolate indeed without her love and devotion. How clearly I remember a conversation that went something like this: "Mamma, will you read to me now? Just a few pages, Mamma."

I would carry a book into the kitchen where my mother was ironing or to the dining room where she sat at her sewing machine. Sometimes I followed her to the back porch where she scrubbed clothes on a washboard. Her explanations that she must first finish her work were always gentle and patient. Never did she raise her voice in anger or impatience. More often than not, she would leave her work only to finish it later in the evening when I was tucked safely into bed. Due to her kindness and tact, I was eight years old before I realized that I was blind.

When a teacher was found to teach me Braille, Mother learned Braille with me. Since we could see the teacher only once a week, Mother felt that my progress would be too slow with so little help, so my education became another of her many tasks. When I did enter a day school for the blind, I was able to

233

go into the fifth grade with the children in my own age group. Had she merely been the traditional busy housewife, this would have been noteworthy enough, but since she was the sole provider for four children, it was remarkable. By taking in washing and sewing, working in the homes of neighbors, and remaking second-hand clothing that friends and relatives contributed, we were able to manage.

My mother was often asked why she did not send me away to school. In those days, practically all blind children attended special state institutions. To such questions Mother would say, "I want Lucile to have the same love and care that my other children have. Now that she has learned to read, we can manage until the class for the blind in Los Angeles is ready."

When the class was finally organized, Mother sold our home in the small town of Compton, where we had always lived, and moved to Los Angeles. This was in 1919, shortly after the close of World War I.

As I made friends with the blind students in my school, we took some of them into our home. There was Marguerite, the little girl whose parents were in the restaurant business and who were busy until late in the evening. Could someone care for the child after school hours until her parents could come for her? I told my mother what the situation was, and Marguerite practically became a member of the family. This resulted in a beautiful friendship for me that will never die. Marguerite became much closer to my mother than to her own, because she was with my mother during the years of adolescence when a girl needs a mother's companionship most.

Since we lived only four blocks from my school, our home became the favorite visiting place for my friends. Mother never minded their noise.

My friends were sure that when they came to our house, refreshments would be in order. Mother's homemade cookies and chocolate cake were always a delight. Whenever there was a school picnic, there were always two or three friends ready to share my lunch with me. Mother's deviled eggs and well-filled sandwiches were always popular.

I could never have finished high school and college without Mother's help. In the late twenties and early thirties, there were very few textbooks to be had in Braille. Mother did most of my reading. She also spent long hours dictating French to me, and I transcribed page after page of it into Braille.

234

Since we had to take in roomers, we never had much privacy as a family. Strangely enough, we didn't mind this too much, because Mother had a way of making them seem a part of the household. They all loved her because she was friendly without intruding in their affairs.

Though Mother was much too busy to attend clubs or have hobbies, she did love to go to shows, both movies and stage plays. We saw some wonderful pictures and plays together. People used to ask my mother how I could enjoy them. "I tell her the pictures and read her the titles on the screen," she answered simply. "The stage plays are easier because she can hear the voices."

When talking movies came in, Mother's task was much easier, and the pictures took on new life. Nevertheless, due to Mother's careful descriptions, I was able to follow the stories of the silent pictures and enjoy them perfectly. Often we could discuss these pictures at home, and Mother would laughingly tell friends that she had tried so hard to make the pictures clear to me that I could tell the story better than she could.

After my sisters and I married, Mother gave up our old home and divided her time among us.

She went to her heavenly home on the thirty-first of December. How fitting that she should start a new life with a new year! Her work on earth was done; she would not have wanted to stay here any longer.

Because of her, I have never known a world of darkness. Because of her, I have been able to live a busy and happy life. With her as my inspiration, I shall continue to do so. As she always has been, she always will be my guiding light.

Relief Society Magazine, October 1956, pp. 670-72.

SOPHY H. VALENTINE*

"The Wind Has Gone"

I often think of an incident that oc-
curred in my childhood and gave me great comfort to dwell
upon.

I was then living with my aunt in Wisconsin on a big farm
three or four miles from Racine. I had no playmates of my own
age. I received private instruction three times a week by the
Danish clergyman, so I did not even have the pleasure and
exhilaration of school life. I was far away from my dear home
and was often very lonely. I had, however, one friend, a girl of
my own age, who lived four miles farther out in the country. To
her I was very much attached, and at her home I spent my happiest days.

It was on my birthday, the 12th of February. I had been
promised that I should be allowed to spend two days at my
friend's and I had looked forward to this for weeks; I had
drowned many a little grief in the hope of this pleasure.

Well, the day dawned at last and I awoke by hearing the
limbs of the apple tree beat violently against the window shut-
ters. My heart sank within me, for I knew that with this terrific

*Sophy H. Valentine was born February 12, 1861, in Denmark to Rasmus and Ane
Christensen Hansen. The mother of four children, she was a Relief Society and temple
worker. She died in Salt Lake City on March 27, 1940.

236

windstorm and the thermometer ten degrees below zero, I would not be permitted to go.

All morning I went about with tearful face, looking despairingly out of the window for a sign of some encouragement in the look of the weather, but the wind kept up its terrible howl and shook the trees till many of them broke. Aunty scolded me for my despondent looks and told me to give it up, as there was no hope of the wind going down from the looks of things.

I went up in the front room and stood shivering with cold, chewing my apron in deepest despair and trying to check the deep sobbing that shook me. Then in my sorrow I dropped on my knees and cried imploringly to the Lord to have pity on me and my loneliness; to let the wind go down that I might go. I ended my prayer by reminding him how Jesus had promised that we should receive whatsoever we asked in his name. Full of faith and courage, I arose and went to the window. The trees shook as if some mighty hand had hold of them, and then suddenly let go. I stood and stared, not daring to breathe. The trees swayed softly to and fro and finally made not a move. I knelt again and whispered a hurried, excited, thanks dear Lord, and then flew into the sitting room. "Aunty! The wind has gone down!"

"No?"

"It has!"

Aunty went to the door and looked out and then exclaimed, "Well, I declare, so it has—I never saw anything like it." I went to my friend's house, of course.

Now, call it childishness if you like, or chance or anything, but it will not rob me of the pleasure I find in putting my own interpretation on it.

If I live to be an old, old woman I shall never forget it, I always thank the Lord, who remembered the poor lonely child though she was not then a member of The Church of Jesus Christ of Latter-day Saints. It shows to me that God is interested in the everyday affairs of his children.

Young Woman's Journal, vol. 8 (1896-97), pp. 313-14.

LENORE BENNION
VINCENT

"No Greater Gift"

When they were married, they knew that all was not well with her, physically. She was so nervous, and her hands shook. The doctor had said it was an overactive thyroid, but the medicine only made her worse. But they married anyway, and then, with a baby on the way, the troubles got much worse. She had to go to the hospital, and they said that the best thing that they could do was to take the life of the baby so that her life could be preserved. Then her thyroid gland would have to be operated on after the baby was taken.

But how could such a decision be made? He had met this beautiful girl in Hamilton, Canada, while they were both yet missionaries for the Church. She had gone home first and they had written such wonderful letters, getting acquainted and sharing their love for the gospel and the Lord. When they had married, they held deep in their hearts the desire to be obedient and to serve the Lord in every way they could. They had both been promised in their patriarchal blessings that they would have children in Zion. They had tried in every way to do what was right, and yet, here was the doctor telling them that their baby would have to die and that, with a thyroid condition as bad as hers, she should never try to have any more children.

How that young husband did pray to the Lord, and how he

searched his own mind for answers! Anxiously, he sought guidance from his own mother and from his sisters. They all felt that it would be the best for him to follow the doctor's advice; that perhaps if the baby were allowed to live, it would be deformed or mentally unbalanced; that the mother might lose her life upon giving birth to the baby even if it were to be normal. He thought and prayed and searched for the right answer. And finally, he gave permission for her to be prepared to go to surgery.

But still, he felt ill at ease. His heart did not feel that this was right, so again he went to her bedside and gave her a special blessing that if it would be the will of the Lord, this baby would not have to die, and that it would be born and his wife would be there to raise it. Then he went to his wife's father and told him what had happened and sought advice. A new answer came to him that had not been presented before; a new avenue that might be the answer to his prayers. This was the advice to get a consultation from another doctor before surgery.

So the next morning, with gown on and all prepared for surgery, she was examined, and her records were examined by not just one other doctor, but two fine members of the Church who were outstanding doctors in this field. And with gratitude in his heart, and tears of joy, he told her that the doctors felt that she could carry the baby until almost full term, and that all would be well.

Christmas passed, January and February came and went, and she improved and was able to be out of the hospital from time to time. Finally, in March, it was felt that the baby was strong enough to make it on its own. So a fine little boy was born. That night, together, they gave thanks to God for this miracle of miracles. They knew they had done the will of the Lord, and they were so grateful that they had not succumbed to the measure of snuffing out a life. And, above all, they were thankful for the faith they had in the healing power of the priesthood.

But soon they wanted more children, and the doctor felt that he should perform an operation on her thyroid before any more children came. A date was set. When that date came, she told the doctor that she was already expecting another baby. Because she was so certain in her faith that all would be well, he performed the operation as planned. Again, her faith was repaid. Since that time, she has lived a good healthy life and has borne four more children.

In this day, when Satan's power is so convincing and so strong, I am glad for this example of courage and faith. We are so bombarded from every side about the population explosion, the rights of women to govern their own bodies, and the freedom of sex, that we must be strong. But with women like this who trust in the Lord, who desire to do what is right, we have a beacon light.

This woman is my mother. I am the fourth of the six children. I am so grateful for this sweet mother and my stalwart father, who chose to serve the Lord, who loved me before I was born, and who desired to bring my brothers and sister into this world and teach me and provide for my exaltation. There is no greater gift to me than this, except that which the Savior gave to us all.

KRISTINE WALKER

"I Found My Mother"

Perhaps, like most teenagers, I have taken my parents' love for granted. I never really considered the immeasurable amount of time, effort, money, or patience they spent on me. Particularly with my mother was this the case.

It seems now that many times I resented my mother, resented things she stood for, things she asked me to do, things she told me about her childhood life. I resented the fact that I, as the eldest of seven children, had all the responsibility, or so I felt. It was up to me to set the example—a word I grew to hate—to lead the way, to try things and get into trouble so that, it seemed, the way was clear for the other children to do just about what they would. I remember how I resented the certain tone of voice Mother used to call me to help her. Certain phrases stand out in my mind, and I can hear the tone even now:

"Kristy, help me with dinner."

"The twins need their shoes cleaned."

"Kristy, Sue and Gay are quarreling; can't you do something?"

"Nancy needs some attention; would you read her a story?"

I always felt like saying "No," but, of course, I didn't.

Then September came and I went away to college. All my younger life the school had carried with it a romantic aura. It was there that my parents met; there they fell in love and were married; there I was born. So I anxiously looked forward to going—for me—"home."

But at that time, in September, there was more to it than that: I wanted to get away from home—my real home. And yet, as time passed and I read my mother's letters telling me about the day-to-day things she did, I began to realize, deep within me, that she gave all her time, money, effort, and thought to her children. I learned that all the meetings, all the shopping, all the housecleaning, all the teaching—actually everything—was directly or indirectly related to serving her family. And all this I learned so slowly and subtly that I barely realized the knowledge was there.

Then one day I came home from my morning classes and found a letter from my mother. It was a simple, ordinary letter, full of the news of home. It told how Dave and Dan, the twins, had flushed a whole roll of tissue paper down the toilet, which flooded over just as Mother was ready to leave for Relief Society. It told of how Mother simply had to find the time to give Sandy a haircut. It told of Mother taking Nancy to dancing lessons, and watching her, and being so proud of her.

It was just a regular, everyday letter, but I had scarcely reached the second page when a feeling suddenly started within me and spread throughout me. It was like the sun bursting from behind a cloud, spreading its sunshine. I could suddenly see my mother as she really was—an unselfish, loving, and celestial being, the person who had done more for me than anyone else, and yet the person to whom I gave the least credit.

I threw myself on my bed and cried; cried with the gladness of the sudden discovery; cried with the unhappiness of my ingratitude and how it had undoubtedly hurt my mother. I quickly wrote her a letter and told her of my love and appreciation for her. It wasn't a good letter, but it was a sincere one, and she wrote back just as quickly:

"Dearest Kristy, I read your letter, and I wept."

New Era, October 1974, p. 27.

◄——————►

WASEL AMELIA BLACK WASHBURN

When I was very, very young I had an experience that made a faith-promoting story for our family, as well as many friends. We lived in Colonia Pacheco, Chihuahua, Mexico, high in the Sierra Madre Mountains. Our home was at the edge of town, with a cornfield and a river nearby. I was the baby of the family and was two and one-half years of age.

My parents would often take me with them in the evenings to the pasture after the cows.

One Sunday in late afternoon, when they started to the pasture, they said I could not go. Mother told me to play with the older children. I turned away, and my parents supposed I would stay, so they started on, but I tried to follow them. They were soon out of sight so I just wandered on.

When Mother returned to the house she could not find me. She inquired and looked all around the place, but to no avail. Becoming alarmed, she went to the barn and told my father I was lost. He, thinking perhaps I would be found asleep nearby, leisurely looked through the house and around the yard and outbuildings. Calling me, Mother ran to the well, the river, and cornfield.

Darkness was coming on and they decided they must have

help. A neighbor was passing by, so Father asked him to go to Sunday evening meeting and notify the congregation and bring help. The bishop announced the tragedy and excused the meeting. The whole congregation went to our home where each in turn looked under the beds, through the house, and around the yard.

By this time, Mother was panicky with fear, because of the many wild animals and other dangers encountered in the mountains.

Under the leadership of my grandfather, John Karchner, groups were organized to begin a thorough search. They agreed that if I were found, a gun would be fired five times to signal the other searchers. The parties circled the place at different distances, carrying pitch pine torches and lanterns to light their way.

Bishop Hardy was with the group that found my tracks where I had crossed a road. By careful observation they were able to follow the tracks for some distance through fields, a patch of corn, and a slough, where they could no longer track me. Here the bishop drew away from the others, kneeled down, and asked the Lord, in faith and sincerity, to guide him to me. As he arose to his feet he thought he heard my voice calling "Mama." He ran in the direction of the sound. After running about a mile and a half he found me trudging wearily along, occasionally calling for Mama in a faint tired voice. He carried me as fast as possible to the appointed place and fired the gun. There he found Mother, who had been waiting since the searching parties left.

They waited until everyone returned, then knelt in a circle, and the bishop poured out thanks to the Lord for protecting me and directing him to me.

His amen was repeated reverently by everyone present.

◄ ● ►

JANE WALTON *

"Posey"

As told by Jessie M. Sherwood

From the Church authorities came a call for Jane Walton's son, Charles, to join with a dozen families, all to leave their comfortable homes in Bluff and make an entirely new settlement in the Blue Mountain region, now known as Monticello, Utah. To issue such a call to Jane's son was equivalent to commanding Jane to go also, for Charles was under twenty, and her mother love would never permit her to see him start for the wilderness alone.

The difficulties of this new settlement were manifold. Because of scant rainfall, dry farming had to be practiced. The altitude of over seven thousand feet caused early frosts. Water for household use was difficult to obtain.

Time passed, and summer came. One day, as Jane was hoeing beans, she was startled to find a young Indian, Posey by name, standing near. Posey didn't bear a very good reputation, and Jane was alone. "Me hungry," said Posey.

"Well," parried Jane, "if you will wait until I finish hoeing this row of beans, I will go into the house and get you some food."

"Me hungry now," reiterated Posey sharply.

*Jane Walton's mother joined the Church in Scotland when Jane was six years of age. Jane walked by her mother's side across the plains in Utah. She died July 24, 1891.

245

"Well," argued Jane, "if you will finish hoeing this row, Posey, I will go at once."

"Me no hoe, and me hungry now," bellowed Posey savagely. Then, pointing his gun at Jane, he swore a volley of terrible oaths.

The insolence and profanity thoroughly angered Jane, who, without a thought of consequences, raised her hoe and hit Posey over the head. He dropped to the ground unconscious. Here was a dilemma! Jane wondered if Posey were dead, but anxious though she was, she kept on with her work. Just as she finished the row she saw, from the corner of her eye, Posey slowly rising. Her heart leaped to her mouth, and she dreaded what he might now do. Just then hoofbeats sounded, and Jane realized that Charles was returning home and the Walton dog was with him. Posey became aware of these sounds too, and realized his game was up. Grasping his gun, with a bloodcurdling whoop, he hurriedly tried to reach his horse but could not move quite fast enough. The dog became very much interested in the seat of Posey's pants, was quite successful in obtaining same, and Posey, sans trousers seat, with another yell, mounted his horse and raced away.

On hearing his mother's story, Charles was gravely concerned, while all the settlers were thrown into consternation, as they feared an Indian attack would be made. Days passed, however, and gradually their fears were forgotten. Weeks later, Posey again came asking for food, and as he slid through the doorway he averred, "Me no mad," which caused Jane and the whole village to be easy in their minds as far as Indians were concerned. Indeed, a deep and lasting friendship sprang into being between the Walton family and the Indians.

Improvement Era, January 1947, pp. 22ff.

◄—◆—►

EMMELINE B. WELLS

"I Have a Testimony to Bear"

I think this is the third fast day that I have made up my mind that I certainly would speak, but did not because—well, there is always somebody ready to speak, and I guess I am not quick enough. I feel that I have a testimony to bear, a testimony that I have always kept from the very day that I entered the city of Nauvoo and saw the Prophet Joseph. He came down to the boat to meet the Saints who were coming from the eastern states and the middle states.

I had been baptized by the wish of my mother, who became a Latter-day Saint as soon as she heard the gospel, but I had no testimony and I had not very much faith. I was always interested in the people who were scholarly and in the greatest schools of the world, and I was particularly happy to believe that I was going to be very great and prominent.

When I came up the river on the boat and stood on the top of the boat to see the Prophet on the landing, I knew instantly then that the gospel was true by the feeling that pervaded me from the crown of my head to the end of my fingers and toes, and every part of my body. I was sure then that I was right, that Mormonism was true and that I was fully paid for all the sacrifices that I had made to come to Nauvoo. I felt that just to see him would be worth it all. I had been prepared in a measure for seeing him, but I want to tell you I was not disappointed, because there never was a man like him.

The only other incident where a man resembled the Prophet was when Brigham Young announced himself as president of the Church and the successor of the Prophet Joseph. I don't remember the words but that was the announcement that he made in the grove on Temple Hill in the city of Nauvoo. There were but very few people that knew he had returned to Nauvoo. They knew all the Twelve were away at the time the Prophet Joseph and his brother Hyrum were slain, and I think very few in that audience knew that Brigham Young had returned.

When he came forward and made that announcement, the whole company arose and exclaimed, in one voice, you might say, that it was the Prophet Joseph. I was standing in a wagon box on wheels, so I did not have to rise, but those who were seated arose and made that exclamation. I could see very well, and everyone thought it was really the Prophet Joseph risen from the dead. But after Brigham Young had spoken a few words the tumult subsided, and the people realized that it was not the Prophet Joseph, but the President of the Quorum of the Twelve Apostles. It was the most wonderful manifestation, I think, that I have ever known or seen, and I have seen a very great number.

It was my privilege when I first went to Nauvoo to be in the homes of Latter-day Saints as soon as I arrived, and the same evening I heard the Prophet Joseph speak to the people. A large number of us had gathered at the Murdock home on Temple Hill. I did not know that the Prophet was coming, but he came that evening. I have never felt anything so very wonderful as that evening when he talked to us. But I did not speak with him, nor did I shake hands with him or go near him, but afterwards I recited for him and sang for him. I was closely associated with people who knew him. Then, when he was taken to the prison, I saw him as he went. I remember very well the day when his body was returned. The heavens poured out rain, just as if the heavens wept over him.

Relief Society Magazine, October 1920, pp. 561-62.

FLO WHITTEMORE[*]

"Helping Hands"

I had not invited her to come into my home that morning. Yet, at nine o'clock, there she was, energetically scrubbing away on my dirty woodwork and looking as cheerful, I thought to myself, as though she enjoyed it.

Why? I questioned almost aloud as I watched her from the davenport where I was lying. Then, as if an effort to discover "why" was too much exertion for a body weakened by illness and a mind weary of trying to solve problems, I said a bit querulously to myself, Oh, well, if she wants to do it, it's perfectly all right! Only I don't see why she should enjoy doing it!

When I had answered her knock on my door that eventful day, she had smiled pleasantly as she asked, "How are you this morning?"

Glad to have anyone come in, I quickly bade her enter. But before I could tell her of my aches and pains and discouragement, she said, "I think you'd better just lie down again and take it easy. You've been pretty sick, you know. I didn't have

[*]Flora Whittemore was born October 10, 1890, in Pleasant Grove, Utah, a daughter of Hosea Brown and Arletta Sterret. The mother of three children, fourteen grandchildren, and nineteen great-grandchildren, she has had some of her writing published in national magazines.

anything in particular to do today, so I thought I'd just slip in here and wash your woodwork and clean your windows for you. I know it must be hard to lie there and look at these things that need doing."

All of a sudden, a spark of interest stirred inside me. "It will be nice," I acknowledged, "to have the windows washed, especially this one in front of me. It's so dirty, everything looks gray outside."

"I know. Almost gives you a gloomy outlook on life, doesn't it?" she replied cheerily as she proceeded to undo the bundle of cloths she had brought.

Hmmm! I thought, *almost!* Why shouldn't I be *altogether* gloomy just lying here day after day? And I retired again into my morbid thoughts.

I became fascinated as I watched her quick, vigorous movements: up and down and across, not a stroke wasted. Lola was like that in everything she did. Without saying a word, she radiated life and good cheer. Deftly, almost gracefully, I thought, she bent to wring the water out of the scrub cloth as she wiped the clean white wood with clear water before polishing it with a dry cloth.

We didn't talk; I was too tired. But it seemed to me only a matter of few minutes until all the woodwork in the living room was spotless.

"It does look better," I acknowledged aloud. "I didn't realize it was so dingy."

"Well, with a coal fire, it doesn't take long," Lola answered as she picked up the pans of dirty water. Then, stepping quickly into the kitchen, she got a smaller pan of clean water and soap and returned to the living room windows.

In a very short while she had both of the windows and the glass in the door so clean and shining that one could almost believe there was no glass in the frames at all!

For the first time since she had come, I think I smiled, and something deep down inside me fluttered ever so slightly. I felt it but refused to give happiness a chance. Instead, I pulled down the corner of my mouth again and turned my face to the wall.

If Lola was disappointed, she gave no sign; but resolutely filling her pans with clean, warm water, she began scrubbing the woodwork in the bedroom, all the while whistling or humming a cheery accompaniment to the rhythmic movements of her hands.

As Lola prepared to leave, I got up to thank her. I expressed appreciation, in a matter-of-fact way, for her efforts to help me, and I was glad to have my house clean, too.

"It was nice of you to do it," I said. And then, as she chatted happily about making some bright ruffled curtains for the kitchen windows, the miracle happened.

I glanced down at the hands that must have been lovely when she came to my house that morning. I could see that they were small and beautifully shaped with tapering fingers that looked more like they should be skimming over piano keys than scrubbing dirty woodwork.

But now they were red, rough, and scratched, the nails cracked and broken—but before I could say a word, Lola was gone.

I knew she did not have to do the menial tasks that she had done so willingly in my home. She had done it for the *love* of me—to help lift me up out of the discouragement and despair into which I had fallen and to give me a new hold on life, she had scrubbed and scoured.

At that moment, it was as though a spring shower had suddenly descended upon my spirit and was cleansing it of all the accumulation of doubt and despair and weakness that had piled up during months of illness.

Relief Society Magazine, October 1956, pp. 673-75.

LaPREAL WIGHT

"There Is Room in Our Inn"

"**I**f you keep my commandments. . ."

And she had kept His commandments.

This thought came to me suddenly and impressively the day Mary Hurren Wight walked into her kitchen with the sick child in her arms. It was not her child, for she was seventy years of age; nor was it the child of her kith and kin. It was the sick child of total strangers, people bogged down with trouble and a broken car, camped under the locust tree at the edge of the lane.

Mary's children rose up in protective alarm.

"Mother! You might be exposing the whole family to something terrible," they remonstrated. "You don't know what the child has. It could have anything!"

"It is not a question of what it has or could have," she answered firmly. "The child is sick. A little baby cannot be sick inside a wretched car—with Mormon homes about it. Every house has a door. Doors were made to let people in. And when has my door ever been shut?"

"We know," they continued. "But there is so much one could do without bringing the child home."

"That's just it," triumphantly replied their mother. "Home—why, this innocent young one has no home! We have a warm, happy one—and there is room at our inn. Besides, in a way these people are strangely close to us, camped as they are under our locust tree. Literally, they are our neighbors."

Linked by common understanding of their mother's purpose, which had always seemed clear and fixed when she was serving for good her fellowmen, the girls' significant glances decided their mother had made the right decision. It may have been, also, that they saw the sick child's face, and with one accord they agreed they should call a doctor.

"Yes, immediately," said Mary, "although there is not much a body can do at this stage. The little soul is so near to making its last earthly flight. I doubt that even a doctor can help." Then she added, slowly, "I think you had better put a bite to eat on the table. The child's mother will be here. She's hungry. Her husband is hungry also. They have been worried, those two. I guess they never thought of food. At least they did not have any. I asked them. Set the table for two."

Mary Hurren Wight was my grandmother, and I never came in close contact with her that I did not realize that I was in the presence of a good woman. But I think I had never known until the following two days just how much strength there is in a beautiful soul. I was to learn it through the eyes of the dead child's mother, for in spite of everything one could do, there was a moment when the baby smiled up at us, gratefully, it seemed, for its warm, clean bed in Mary's kitchen; then, with a little sigh of such sweet content, it closed its eyes peacefully, and its soul winged homeward.

Later, husband and wife approached Mary, their hands clasped together, his arm laid consolingly about his partner's shoulder. There was a mystified horror in his eyes, and his speech was awkward and hesitant in its despair.

"Could we . . . would we be able to . . . well, his mother and I would like a little sermon preached before we bury him. Would it cost too much?"

"Not a penny," Mary promised them with that peculiar knowledge of things that seemed to place her so essentially apart from the rest of us. "My church does not take money for preaching."

As she continued to explain to them our beliefs, I saw the fear leave their faces, and in its place adoration for this aged woman lit up their countenances, and they appeared gallant in their sorrow. I felt that throughout their years no one had stopped to be kind to them before. And they were the type that needed kindness. They had probably needed it many times along their way. If someone had lent a hand, they might never have had to face the sorrow that was theirs to bear at that moment.

When I heard the simple voices of neighbors ring out in song—a funeral hymn—in Mary's front parlor, and saw the humble, grateful tears in the eyes of the still bewildered parents as they looked upon the little pine box, made by other neighbors' hands; when I smelled the faint odor of Mary's garden flowers adding color to the casket, making it appear beautiful and fragrant; when I heard the bishop speak of life eternal, I was proud of my grandmother, for I realized she had brought this good moment about, and my soul went on its knees to her. I was a witness to the keeping of the greatest of all commandments, as our Father in heaven intended it to be kept.

"And, if you keep my commandments and endure to the end. . . ." (D&C 14:7.)

My grandmother endured to the end. She was as old as a tree; her eyes could no longer see clearly the beauties of her labor: the flowers she had planted, the winding of her old English clock, the food she had helped to preserve. Her feet no longer took her to the places she wanted to go: to the sick and the troubled, to her church, and to the last resting place at the foot of the mountains, where seven of her thirteen children lay buried. But she never faltered in her desire to live the way God wanted her to live.

Improvement Era, August 1953, p. 571.

HOPE M. WILLIAMS

"Grafted"

"**P**ut' er here! It's gonna be a homer! Home it!"

These cries reached Janet's ears as she sat at her desk near the window. She lifted her head from her books to see her young nine-year-old son, Ronnie, slide free into home plate. A smile lingered on her face as she watched the tickled way he picked himself up, brushed off his pants, and received the well-earned pats on the back from the boys on his team. His face was damp and dusty, and one whole side of his pants was solid dirt despite the dusting routine, but the grin on his face showed pure joy.

I'm glad I didn't have that lot plowed for a garden, Janet thought, although it would have helped with the groceries. And Ronnie was so happy to have the boys come here to play. Besides, she confessed to herself, a garden is just too hard for me to take care of alone. She dismissed these thoughts from her mind and went back to the clippings and pictures before her.

Janet had been trying to get courage enough to work on her book of remembrance for some time, but she could never quite get beyond the starting process. Just seeing some familiar thing of her husband's—a letter or a picture—brought back that painful tightness in her chest, so the boxes of clippings would be put away to await a braver day. This seemed to be that day, for she had finished several pages in the ancestry section, copying their family group sheet again in black ink, remembering to write the word "adopted" after Ronnie's name, and to follow carefully the line across to record the date of his sealing. She had even been able to fill in the marriage and endowment dates opposite her husband's name, and with a steady hand, the date in the deceased column, 25 November 1954.

How close David seems to me today, Janet mused; almost as though he were actually with us again. And that's the way it should be, she concluded calmly, as she pasted in a picture of herself and David beside Ronnie's picture.

It had been nearly six years since the terrible accident that had taken David's life and from which she and Ronnie, both badly bruised and broken, had miraculously survived. They had had only eight years of married life, and Ronnie had been with them just four short years when the tragedy occurred.

What a long time ago it seems, she thought, when the Child Welfare Department of the Relief Society called to tell us about our baby. In her memory Janet was back again with her husband on that never-to-be-forgotten day when they had brought Ronnie home. How sweet he was and how precious! How his little hand would fold about her outstretched finger! Could any parents have been more proud? Could any parents have prayed more fervently for their child than we did? She wondered.

As she leafed through more pictures and papers and thought of that happy time, she noticed a poem that she had clipped from a magazine at a time when they had still been waiting for their adopted child. The poem was entitled "To a Foster Child." She read it through, thinking as she did how accurately the author had portrayed the emotion she had so often felt but had been unable to express. She read the last lines aloud, enjoying the rhythm and the poetry of the words:

> ... The days have lengthened, listening
> Toward your voice somewhere crying ...
> The barren stalk seeks out its blossom,
> Choice between wholeness and dying.
> Let bone of bone, let flesh of flesh be part,
> For stock, like seed, may fruit.
> Love flowers fiercely in the heart
> Grafted to heart by need.[1]

---

[1]Grace Maddock Miller, *McCall's*, April 1941. Reprinted by permission of *McCall's*.

"Grafted by need," she replied. "That's a beautiful comparison!"

Bang! The whole house shook as Ronnie burst into the room, and Janet's reverie was abruptly interrupted.

"I'll never play with those kids again! I hate 'em all!" The words exploded from Ronnie as he bolted through the sunny kitchen and through the hall to his own bedroom, where he again slammed the door. Silence followed; then Janet could hear sounds of muffled sobbing.

Oh, dear, she thought, feeling that familiar pain—and they were playing so nicely together, too. I wonder what went wrong. Silently she prayed, Don't let him be hurt too much—not again; I can't bear it.

"Ronnie—what's the matter, honey?"

"Nothin'," came the angry voice. "Just go away and leave me alone!"

Janet winced at the rebuff but decided that it would be best to do as he said, so she picked up the things from the table, the mood for reminiscing and working on books having vanished when the storm cloud in the form of a small boy burst in.

Half an hour had gone by when Janet heard Ronnie's door open, and the tear-stained face of her boy appeared.

"Those kids gone yet?" he mumbled as he started outside. " 'Cause I sure don't want 'em around playing cars with me!" And without waiting for an answer, he went out to the familiar dirt pile where he spent so many hours alone building roads and dugways and playing with his beloved friends—the cars and trucks.

Janet let him play while she prepared supper, purposely keeping busy so that she could remain calm, and when it began to grow dark she was able to affect an almost cheerful quality in her tone as she called, "Hey, chum, your supper is ready now, okay?"

"Okay," he answered simply and began picking up his playthings.

During the meal Janet tried to make conversation, talking cheerfully about small things and acting unconcerned, but Ronnie remained silent. The dark anger was gone from his brown eyes now, and only the hurt and sadness remained. Finally, Ronnie brought his eyes up from the untouched food on his plate and began hesitantly, "Mom, do you know why I said for you to go away? To leave me alone?"

"Oh," Janet smiled at him, "I just thought it was because boys want to be alone sometimes."

"No—not 'specially. It was—well, you know what we both said—that it was against the rule to cry about Daddy."

"Oh. Were you crying about Daddy?"

"Well, sort of. You see, we got to talking about going on the fathers' and sons' outing. And then—the kids said that I couldn't go 'cause I didn't have a father. And I told 'em I did, too, have a father but he was up in heaven. And then Tommy said—that—how could my father take me camping if he was up in heaven? And then, I said that maybe Mr. Owens would take me like he did last year. And then Larry—you know Larry, Mamma—he said that my daddy up in heaven wasn't my real daddy anyway 'cause I was adopted. And so—and then—I just told those kids to go home 'cause I was afraid I was about to cry!" And Ronnie's eyes filled again at the remembered injustice.

How cruel children are, Janet thought, as she sought for the right words to comfort him.

"But, sweetheart, you already knew you were adopted. I've told you about that—how your real daddy and mother couldn't take care of you, and how Daddy and I went to get you because we wanted you and needed you so very much."

"Uh-huh, I know. But I didn't stop to think about how I might have a real daddy somewhere." Ronnie was silent, wondering.

"I don't think the boys meant to be unkind, dear," said Janet. "You see, sometimes, it makes people feel important to be able to brag about having something others don't have. Each of those boys has always had his daddy," Janet was very dangerously close to tears herself, "and none of them can know how much we miss ours every single day—and most of all for special things like hunting, or on Christmas, or for fathers' and sons' outings—" Her voice broke and she couldn't go on.

"Don't cry, Mommy. Remember, crying about Daddy is against the rule!"

"Yes, I know." Janet wiped her eyes and smiled at her son. "But I sort of break the rule sometimes, don't you?"

"I sure do!" he replied. Then thoughtfully, he added, "But I'm still not gonna' like those kids—especially Larry!" And with this parting remark he went to prepare for his bath and bed.

Janet's eyes were wet as she picked up the dishes. It isn't

fair to have him hurt like that! I can stand it for myself but not for him. Her thoughts went back to the events of the afternoon—how happy she had felt about everything. And to have it end like this! Suddenly the words "grafted by need" came so clear to her mind that it was almost as though someone had spoken them. Peace filled her heart, and she smiled.

Janet turned down the covers on his bed; then she brought him a glass of milk, knowing that he would be hungry for that, anyway. Always she found herself doing small things for his comfort, trying in some way to make up to him for the hurt he had received.

As Ronnie climbed into bed and received his usual goodnight kiss, he opened the subject again, unexpectedly.

"But, Mom, how come? If I have a real daddy somewhere, why couldn't he be here with us?"

Janet settled herself on the foot of his bed, smiled, and because the answer had been given to her, said calmly, "Honey, you've been taught in Primary and Sunday School about our first parents, and so you know that all living things have parents, don't you?"

"I know. But does everything, Mommy? Even the trees and flowers?"

"Yes, dear, every living thing has parents, but only two. And that's what I want to talk to you about. Do you remember that apple tree in Grandpa's orchard—the one that always has two different kinds of apples on it?"

"You mean that pretty one? And one of its branches has pinker blossoms than the others?"

"That's the one."

"I always liked that tree. And the apples are real good, too." His brown eyes brightened thoughtfully, and he went on to add, "But I like to climb that little short apple tree in the corner, 'cause its branches grow kinda' close to the ground and you can climb it real easy clear up past the place where it was cut off and Grandpa painted it, and then sit in the shady place where all the branches grow out together all thick."

Janet's face showed her pleasure that Ronnie had mentioned the other tree as she hastened to explain, "I'm glad you like that tree, honey, because it's part of the story, too.

"These two trees—the pretty one with different blossoms, and the little short one with thick branches—are very special trees in Grandpa's orchard. Once, both of these trees were having a very hard time to grow. When the short tree was young, a branch grew out from its trunk too soon, and as the little branch grew, it bent the trunk of the tree so much that Grandpa was sure the tree couldn't grow straight if he let it keep growing that way; it would be bent over because its trunk wasn't strong enough yet to bear a branch.

"Now, the tree with the different kinds of blossoms on it didn't always have branches like it does now, either. The branches it did have were all growing on one side of the tree, making it unbalanced, and Grandpa knew that this tree needed another strong branch so that it would grow straight.

"Now, Grandpa is a good gardener. He knew what to do for both of those trees to make them grow straight and strong, and blossom, and bear fruit. So, he cut the one sturdy branch from the little young tree and grafted it into the empty space on the other tree, making sure that he sealed the bark around the graft so that the sturdy little branch would become as much a part of that tree as if it had always grown there. Then, when the little branch was cut from the young tree, the trunk of that tree straightened out and grew and developed and bloomed like it does today."

"Gee, Mom, I think that's real neat!" Ronnie was pleased at the happy ending. "Grandpa was such a good gardener that he saved both of the trees and the little branch, too, huh?"

"Yes." Janet's voice reflected her gratitude that her son had understood the real meaning of her story, and she added very tenderly, "Our Heavenly Father is the very best Gardener of all, and he grafted you from the tree of the parents who started your growth, right into the empty place on our family tree just like Grandpa did with that little branch; and when we went to the temple and had you sealed to us, that's how our Heavenly Father sealed the graft and made you our very own little boy, and made us your parents."

The ball games went on as usual as the days passed, and the boys seemed to be the best of friends. As Janet trimmed the edges of the lawn, she could hear them talking, and out of the corner of her eye she saw Ronnie toss the ball nonchalantly into the air, catch it with one hand, straighten his cap, and say, "You know what? Mr. Owens asked me to go on the outing again. You know, I call him 'Daddy Ken' all the time—'cause he doesn't have a boy—and my dad isn't here either, so we just pretend. It's lots of fun. When it's time to go to bed, 'Daddy Ken' always says, 'Well, son, let's hit the sack!' And I say, 'Okay,' Just like that. It's real neat, I think!"

"But gee whiz, Ronnie!" countered Larry, "that's just pretending! We're all going with our own dads. Don't you wish you were like us?"

Janet's throat tightened in apprehension as she listened for Ronnie's answer.

"Not any more, I don't," Ronnie bragged. "You see, it's like this. I was grafted from an apple tree, and now my daddy in heaven is my real daddy—and my mom is my real mother—'cause their tree needed a branch more than the little tree in the corner. It grew lots of branches after I was cut off, so it doesn't need me anymore, but my mom's tree sure does!"

Janet smiled as she saw the boys' mystified looks, and as she picked up her trimmers she heard Tommy say, "Yeah, I guess your Mom does need you now, Ronnie. 'Specially since your Daddy isn't here. But, c'mon, you guys, let's play ball!" And as Janet opened the door to go inside, she heard Larry's muttered exclamation, "An apple tree! Good grief!"

After Ronnie was asleep, Janet lay thinking of all that had happened, and she couldn't help but smile as she remembered Ronnie's mixed-up, but wise, explanation. Much later, still unable to sleep, she got up and looked out of the window at the peaceful, starlit sky.

"It's all right, David," she whispered. "Our boy is growing strong to our family tree. Now he understands, also, darling, that 'love flowers fiercely in the heart, grafted to heart by need.'"

Relief Society Magazine, January 1961, pp. 17-22.

ROSE MARIE WINDER

"Kathy"

We're a Latter-day Saint family of five and reside near Atlanta, Georgia: my husband, Richard, who was born into the Church; myself, a convert who was baptized two weeks before our wedding day in Salt Lake City, Utah; Parry, seventeen, and Mike, fourteen, both blessed with strong healthy bodies and minds, involved in football, baseball, and other sports; and Kathy, eleven. We're a happy family because we have the gospel in our home.

At eleven, Kathy is quite a girl. She has had a horse for nearly two years and has taken very good care of him. She named him Flapjack. Together they've been in seven shows and have won thirteen ribbons. Kathy works him, bathes him, brushes and primps and fusses with him, and loves him dearly. During the summer months she prefers, more than anything else, to spend her time at the stables. It's a safe place and the children are watched over by the manager and others who work there.

On a beautiful day in May 1974, Dick took Kathy over to the stables at about eleven in the morning with her sack lunch. At about four P.M., I was talking on the phone to a friend when an operator interrupted our conversation to say that there was

°Rose Marie Winder was converted to the Church in Salt Lake City. She and her family reside in Dunwoody, Georgia, where her husband is president of the Sandy Springs Georgia Stake.

an emergency. Immediately we hung up, and one second later the phone rang. It was the manager at the stables, informing me that Kathy and her horse had been hit by a car.

Struggling to keep my voice controlled, I asked, "How bad is she?"

"I don't know," he replied.

I said I would be right there, and hung up. It was the first time in years that I'd been without a car. What to do? First I called Dick at the stake center and told him about the accident; then I called some nonmember friends and asked them to drive me to the stables. They came in five minutes.

When we arrived at the stables, the first thing I saw was the car involved in the accident, with the windshield completely smashed. My heart raced. Many people were waiting to tell us that the ambulance had taken our precious little girl to the hospital. The young man who was driving wanted to tell me he was sorry and hadn't meant to hit Kathy and Flapjack. I was in a hurry and said I'd talk to him later, but now I needed to get to my daughter. As we pulled out of the stable area, Dick arrived and I told him we were on our way to Northside Hospital.

At the emergency ward of the hospital my little girl started to cry when she saw me. I started to cry also, but the nurse on duty (bless her) said, "Please don't—it would be very bad for Kathy." She was right and I knew it, so I took a deep breath to control myself. I needed to be strong so Kathy could get strength from my strength.

Her right ankle was heavily bandaged, the nerves in her neck were twitching badly, and she was shivering. Dick called President Day, his second counselor, and he was there in ten minutes with consecrated oil; then they anointed Kathy and blessed her.

For two hours two orthopedic specialists worked on Kathy's ankle, after which a neurosurgeon checked her out. Then, at about 10:30 P.M., she was finally admitted to a hospital room.

During the long wait, we heard the story in bits and pieces from those who had come from the stables to be with us. Kathy had been on a trail by the tennis court when something spooked her horse and he galloped off quickly. She tried to run him in a circle to slow him down, but he pulled toward the street where a car was coming. Being a jumper of sorts, Flapjack tried to jump over the car's hood. However, the car was coming too fast, and the horse's right side hit the windshield, as did Kathy's right side. She was thrown unconscious to the ground.

Immediately after the accident another car came along and stopped, and a young couple got out to see what had happened. The woman was Kathy's favorite schoolteacher! She called the ambulance and stayed with Kathy until it came. Then another young woman from the stables rode in the ambulance with Kathy to the hospital, so she would be with someone she knew. If I had to, I couldn't have chosen two better persons to be there to help my daughter.

In addition to the badly damaged ankle (which was embedded with glass fragments, dirt, and bone chips, with a piece of bone broken from the anklebone), Kathy had a hairline fracture of the skull above her right ear and a fracture of the right elbow. A bone specialist told us there was a 100 percent chance that the ankle would become infected and that she would be in a wheelchair for some time, then on crutches.

But Kathy never had any infection. She did have to be in a wheelchair for a few days after we brought her home from the hospital and then on crutches for two days. She also had a great desire to get back on her horse as soon as possible—Flapjack had received just two small cuts and a very small puncture on his right side. The fact that the horse was all right was a miracle in itself, because Kathy loves him so much.

Her first Sunday home from the hospital was Fast Sunday, and in fast meeting she was the first person to stand and thank her Heavenly Father for her blessings. She probably won't need plastic surgery on her ankle, her elbow is well healed, and she has now been released by the neurosurgeon. All is well with Kathy. The doctors are amazed at her marvelous and quick recovery. But we, her family, know what miracles can be accomplished through the priesthood of God for those who have faith.

Biographical Sketch

MARVEL YOUNG

Marvel Murphy Young was born in Ogden, Utah, a daughter of Castle H. and Verna Ann Fowler Murphy. When she was seven years old, her father was called to be president of the Hawaiian Mission, and she lived with her parents in the mission home at Kalihi for five and a half years. At the age of nine she was called to be a Primary teacher and as secretary of the Kalihi Branch Primary.

When her father was called to be president of the Hawaiian Temple in 1937 she again went with her parents to Hawaii and lived for three years near the temple in Laie. Although she was just a teenager, she had the special experience of serving as a guide on the temple grounds.

Marvel attended schools in Hawaii and Ogden and was graduated in 1943 from Weber College in Ogden. She served a mission to the Eastern States and then attended Brigham Young University, where she was elected vice president of the student body. On May 31, 1947, she was married to the student body president, Kay A. Young, in the Logan Temple. They have four children and four grandchildren. The Youngs now reside in Orem, Utah.

In the Church she served five years on the Primary general board; she is currently a member of the Youth Correlation Committee.

MARVEL YOUNG

"I Felt Too Much Good Inside"

As a little girl, I lived for five years in the Kalihi Mission Home in Honolulu, Hawaii, while my father was the mission president. Being privileged to associate with missionaries every day, naturally the preaching of the true gospel became extremely important to me. It was amazing to me that everyone who heard this great message didn't immediately embrace it and become a member of the restored church of Jesus Christ, for I knew beyond any shadow of doubt that it was true.

During the summers, when I was not attending school, I busied myself about the mission home, picking hibiscus to beautify it and going on errands for the missionaries. I had the most fun when I helped our Chinese cook, Lau Ah You, as he prepared the large meals for our family and the many missionaries. I learned much about Ah You during those times with him.

Ah You had a wife and six children in China and had come to Hawaii as a young man in order to earn more wages to provide for his beloved family. When he first came to Hawaii, he was hired as the cook for the mission home. Not being able to understand English, he would become very upset when the missionaries would come into his kitchen, and he would fiercely chase them out with his big butcher knife. Slowly, as he began to understand English and he realized that they were not trying to hurt or bother him, he became more friendly with them.

One day when I was helping Ah You with the evening meal, I asked him how many years he had been the mission cook. He said, "Thirty." I asked, "Then why aren't you a Mormon?" He replied, in his pidgin English, "Nobody been speak me."

I just could not imagine that in his thirty years as mission cook, associating with missionaries every day, no one had ever thought of preaching the gospel to Ah You!

I told him about Joseph Smith and his vision; then I quickly went to my father and asked that someone be assigned to teach Ah You the gospel. My father knew that he would understand the gospel better if it were preached to him in his own tongue. Consequently, he organized a group of fine Chinese members of the Church, headed by Brother Henry W. Aki, to meet with Ah You each week in order that he might have a group of his own to belong to and be able to hear the gospel in his own language. (This was the first time that the Chinese had been organized in any Church group anywhere in the world. When President Heber J. Grant came to Hawaii in 1935 and saw how successful this group had become, Elder Matthew Cowley of the Council of the Twelve was sent to China to dedicate that land for the preaching of the gospel.)

After meeting with this group and gaining an understanding of the gospel, Ah You was baptized a member of the Church and was confirmed by my brother, C. Keola Murphy, who was a missionary at the time.

Prior to his baptism, when Ah You attended our missionary testimony meetings, he noticed that some of the missionaries cried, and especially that tears always flowed when my mother bore her testimony. One Sunday morning after meeting, Ah You said, "Sister Murphy, why you all-a-time cry?" She explained to him that when the Spirit bears witness to one's soul of the truthfulness of the gospel, one is filled with warm emotion, and that it is sometimes difficult to keep the tears from flowing. Ah You said, with a shake of his head, "Chinese never cry!"

Later, after he had been baptized, this Chinese group had a lovely affair to honor Ah You as a new member of the Church. They asked that he express himself, and as he did so, tears flowed down his cheeks. After the meeting my mother said, "Ah You, I thought Chinese never cried." He replied, "Ah, but Sister Murphy, I feel too much good inside!"

◆—————◆

"Gospel Teaching"

The far-reaching effect of a good teacher has been very impressive to me. President David O. McKay once said: ". . . children who, through instruction from noble teachers, become imbued with eternal principles of truth, radiate an influence for good, which, like their own souls, will live forever."

My mother, Verna Fowler Murphy, was one such noble teacher. From her earliest years, she had a burning testimony of the gospel and was able, even as a teenager, to express it well. She was especially good at teaching little children about the Savior and his gospel in a way that impressed them deeply. She loved to teach Sunday School and Primary children, never realizing that her teaching would help her own unborn daughter in the years to come.

One of the little children in her Sunday School class in Ogden, Utah, was Johnny Emmett. He was so thrilled with her stories of the Savior that he would go home crying to his mother, saying how wonderful the gospel was and how much he loved the Savior.

At Christmastime, she told them the story "The Other Wise Man," by Henry Van Dyke. The next day, Johnny's mother called my mother and told her how impressed he had been with the story, and how he cried as he told her that he wanted to be like the Other Wise Man and to help others in every possible way when he grew up.

Years later, I was laboring in the Eastern States Mission, in Binghamton, New York. One day, as my companion and I were tracting and receiving many rejections, we became very dejected. When we were about to give up for the day, I was impressed that we should knock on just one more door. We did so, and when a lady appeared at the door, I told her that we represented The Church of Jesus Christ of Latter-day Saints, more commonly called the Mormon Church. She immediately threw open her door and invited us in so quickly that my companion and I looked at each other in amazement.

After we were seated, she explained that if we had come to her door a year before, she would never have allowed us to enter, because she had been a devout Catholic and had not wanted to listen to missionaries from any other church. However, a sad experience in the last six months had changed her thinking, especially concerning the Mormons. She said that her husband had just passed away at the Mayo Clinic in Rochester, Minnesota. He had been attended by a Mormon doctor at the clinic, who had done everything in his power to help her husband to live. He had also gone the extra mile to help her to have faith in the Lord, in spite of their many problems.

She said, "That doctor was an active member of your church; he taught classes every week in the church there, besides being so busy helping everyone medically. He truly lived as the Savior would want us all to live. I feel that any church that could teach a man to be as wonderful as that doctor was must surely be wonderful, too. I am now ready to listen to anything you have to teach me."

My companion and I were thrilled, and before we began to teach her the gospel, we asked the name of the doctor who had inspired her so greatly. She said, "His name was Dr. John L. Emmett, of Ogden, Utah."

Truly, the effects of my Mother's gospel teaching in Sunday School had affected at least one little child so deeply that he radiated the spirit of the gospel by the way he lived. He impressed all whom he knew with his fine example. Without knowing it, he had also helped two lady missionaries find a "golden contact," transforming a discouraging day into a thrilling one. Surely we were led by the Spirit to that special door on that very special day!

SYLVIA PROBST YOUNG *

"The Sky Is Blue Again"

On a day in late autumn, when the clouds hung oppressively low and a mournful wind cried through the bare, brown trees, I closed my door and walked hurriedly across the field to the home of a friend. My thoughts as I walked along were dark as the day. I was lonely, disappointed, sick at heart, feeling that life had hurt me more than I could bear. Nothing seemed really worthwhile anymore. I needed to talk to someone—I wanted sympathy—and so I went to see a woman who is my friend. She was in her little garden behind the house, digging some carrots for the soup she was making.

"It's the kind of a day for good, homemade vegetable soup," she exclaimed, after greeting me warmly. "Come in. I have a nice fire and we can talk."

I apologized for coming so unexpectedly, but she quickly said, "Friends don't need previous appointments; it's a compliment to have you come whenever you will."

Sitting on her worn divan, I talked and she listened, sitting close beside me. With her eyes deep with feeling and understanding, she heard my bitterness and heartache; she shared my tears. Her hand, rough from work and knotted by arthritis, lay

---

*Sister Young has published extensively in Church magazines. She and her husband, Reid Young, are the parents of four sons.

gently on mine. I felt her strength, the comfort she gave without saying a word—she who had known so much of sorrow herself.

When the soup was done, she brought it in on a tray, with homemade bread and apricot marmalade, and I thought it was the best lunch I had ever had.

Too quickly the hour passed, and it was time for me to go. I didn't want to, but I knew that I must. At the door I put an arm around her. "Thank you," I said. "I feel so much better now. Could you possibly know how much you have helped me?"

"I don't know why," she said. "I never seem to know what to say—all I can do is listen and try to understand."

Then she raised her eyes upward. "Oh, look!" she exclaimed brightly. "The sky is blue again; tomorrow will be a better day."

Looking up, I saw that she was right. A big patch of blue was pushing the clouds away, and a ray of sunlight gleamed down.

Walking back home with a new perspective, I thought how infinitely wise she was without knowing it.

"I just listen and try to understand," she had said, but oh, the strength she gave in the listening! For to listen is the highest compliment one can give another—to listen and to understand. How rare and precious is a listener!

Her words at parting had given me much to think about: "The sky is blue again." Certainly all things pass away—sorrow, just as cloudy skies, cannot last indefinitely. "Tomorrow will be a better day."

Yes, tomorrow would be a better day because of the selflessness, the charity, of a wonderful friend.

Relief Society Magazine, March 1968, p. 290.

AUTHOR UNKNOWN

"I'll Pull the Handcart for You"

In the rear part of the company, two men were pulling one of the handcarts, assisted by one or two women. When the cart arrived at the bank of the river, one of these men, who was much worn down, asked, in a plaintive tone, "Do we have to go across there?" On being answered yes, he was so much affected that he was completely overcome. That was the last strain. His fortitude and manhood gave way. He exclaimed, "Oh dear, I can't go through that," and burst into tears. His wife, who was by his side, had the stouter heart of the two at that juncture and she said soothingly, "Don't cry, Jimmy. I'll pull the handcart for you."

As they crossed the river, the sharp cakes of floating ice below the surface of the water struck against the shins of the immigrant, inflicting wounds that never healed until he arrived at Salt Lake, and the scars of which he bears to this day.

Orson F. Whitney, *History of Utah*, vol. 1 (Salt Lake City: George Q. Cannon & Sons Co., 1892), p. 563.

◀━━▶

ANONYMOUS

"That Others May Know"

What does life hold for an active Latter-day Saint who marries a person of another faith or one who feels he "does not need religion"? Without having lived through the experiences this course of action brings, one could guess, perhaps, but never really know.

I know. I have been married under these circumstances for twenty years, and in that time I have felt many emotions and experienced many things.

Because I feel deeply for anyone facing the decision of whether or not to date a nonmember, or whether or not to marry a nonmember with the hope of conversion, let me draw back the curtain and reveal pictures from my married life—happenings one cannot foresee, reactions one cannot guess, dimensions of emotion one can never know without actual experience or without looking through the eyes and listening to the tunes played on the heartstrings of another who has experienced such a marriage.

I was a sophomore student at a Utah university; so was he. We met in a psychology class. I was impressed with his intellect, his bearing, his ambitious, progressive attitude.

We began to date. I thought it would be a casual relationship. I didn't intend that anything serious should come of it. I was an active Church member and had no intention of marrying out of my faith.

When I came to love Fred, nothing doubting, I rationalized that I was not "throwing over" my excellent home and church training. I was naive enough to believe that because he attended church with me and seemed very interested, within a few months he would be converted. Because I believed the principles of the gospel wholeheartedly myself and found them so logical and workable, I thought that anyone with any degree of intelligence would soon be converted, and that when the Holy Ghost bore witness to him, the truth of it would be confirmed to him. Suffice it to say that at this point in life my experience with nonmembers had been practically nil.

Each courtship is so individual, yet I am sure there are common tendencies, one of the strongest of which is for the young couple to be firmly convinced that their "special love" is the most unique, the most sincere, the deepest yet known to man, that without doubt it can surmount any problem. Oh, the yearning of young hearts is most poignant!

Counselors and relatives entreated me to postpone marriage until he had had an opportunity to investigate the gospel thoroughly and the outcome had been determined. My mother endeavored to help me see that she had nothing against him personally, in fact, liked him very much, but with two different sets of basic values we would run into difficulty sooner or later and both be hurt.

We decided to marry—on certain conditions. The conditions I set down were: (1) We were to be married by a Latter-day Saint bishop; (2) our children were to be trained in the LDS faith and baptized members when of age; (3) I was free to serve in callings in my church; (4) the Word of Wisdom was to be practiced in our home. These stipulations were major in my mind, and they were a sacrifice on Fred's part inasmuch as the first two were in direct opposition to the faith he espoused and caused his excommunication from his church. I reasoned that my sacrifice was waiting for a while for a temple marriage.

I am grateful to Fred that he kept his agreement to refrain from interfering with my activity in the Church. I have held many callings through the years, and my bishops and stake presidents have called me to positions that required a minimum of attention during the hours Fred was at home. Thus, I have grown in understanding and deep love of the gospel through my activity.

At various times Fred displayed an interest in the gospel. He went through the missionary lessons three different times, only to turn away afterwards. Once in a while he halfheartedly attended church with us. For most of our married life we have lived in the same friendly ward, and our friends have loved him, prayed for him, and carried him in their hearts as they have gone through the temple. As a family we have loved him, invited him to go with us, showed boundless delight when he accepted but tried to be pleasant when he refused, tried not to exert pressure upon him. Perhaps the latter is hard to achieve, for surely our yearning could not be masked.

It is impossible to describe the emotions that well up within you as you rise each Sunday morning, prepare the children and yourself for church services, and look once more before leaving your bedroom at your husband who is still sleeping or, having risen, is sitting with a morning cup of coffee and the newspaper and seemingly couldn't care less that he is not part of the family group departing for church. It is one of the loneliest feelings I've ever known and to which familiarity lends no softening.

It is emphasized more so when your eldest son, who now holds the priesthood, sets his alarm clock, arises, and goes off alone to priesthood meeting faithfully Sunday after Sunday. What are his thoughts and what does he feel as he sees other boys arriving in the company of their fathers?

With this feeling of tumult in your heart, you find your seat in church and with the opening announcements hear there is to be a temple excursion or an elders party. You know again the yearning realization that you are necessarily excluded because of lack of priesthood and temple marriage. As your eyes wander over the congregation to the faces of your friends, you realize they are included, and you sense their incomparable sense of peace, of oneness, of belonging, in contrast to your own limitations.

It would be a herculean task to find words to convey your frustration and emptiness when, upon finding in a Relief Society or Primary lesson a beautifully taught truth, you desire to share it with your mate and he answers, "I don't care to talk about it," or "I've never thought of that and don't care to now," or still worse, "Someday the crazy things you believe will drive me out of my mind!"

Have you thought of your despair when your sick child cries out in faith in the night for a blessing from the priesthood, and your husband stands by, helpless and unqualified?

Think of fast day or occasions that call for a special fast when you must prepare food for your mate and he feels inclined to flaunt before you his appetite. How would you train your children to observe the principles of the kingdom when one parent does one thing and one another? Have you considered how you would explain your mate's behavior to your children without making them lose respect for him? It is indeed a touchy, delicate responsibility. I say responsibility because it cannot be ignored if you are to teach them gospel principles.

What would you do if your husband saw nothing wrong in taking his sons to a Sunday ball game or movie, thus failing to keep the Sabbath day holy?

Here again it is evident that different basic values in parents cause conflict, making necessary a stream of constant decisions that would be unnecessary if unity of purpose reigned.

Also, it is true that one does not marry just his or her mate, but the beloved's family as well. It is useless to believe they will hold sacred the things you believe when your beliefs are at variance with theirs. Let me illustrate. Having been reared in a home where gracious consideration of guests knew no bounds, I happily, trustingly invited my in-laws to visit us, only to have one of my children whisper to me, "Grandmother says she feels sorry for me because I was born of a Mormon mother! What does she mean? What is wrong with that?"

After one such visit, I found apostate Mormon literature had been placed in the hands of my eldest child. As like incidents continued I felt that my loving hospitality had been betrayed. Fred said he was ashamed of his parents' behavior but he made no effort to set them straight. It became my task to undo the damage of each situation patiently with the help of Heavenly Father.

Reluctantly, I had to admit that as much as I desired and needed a sweet family relationship with my in-laws, they were enemies to the children and me—enemies in a different camp who sought every opportunity to thwart my children's testimonies of the gospel. This called up another responsibility—to teach the children to love their grandparents but to disregard their attempts to defeat their testimonies. What a paradoxical assignment!

Occasionally I have been privileged to attend general conference in Salt Lake City. Once I waited one evening for friends who were going through the temple. As I stood there alone, I felt a failure because of the choice I had made when young. My heart was full of regret, which was all the harder to bear because I knew I had only myself to blame.

As a young woman I had held to a strict standard of never dating young men whose standards were not the best. Fred and I had dated for quite some time, and I had found him to be clean in every respect. There was no smoking, foul language, drinking, or anything but the best of behavior until one night at a college dance. When he took me in his arms to dance, I thought I smelled liquor on his breath. At first I couldn't be sure, so I waited until I was certain. My heart sank, but I knew what I must do. I had so looked forward to this special date, but I told Fred that he must take me home. He looked shocked and inquired why, and I replied that I had always adhered to the standard of not dating anyone who drank intoxicating beverages. He apologized, pointing out that he certainly was not drunk, that he had indulged in only one cocktail before leaving the fraternity house. I insisted that he take me home. On the way I told him I would have to break the dates we had made for the future. I could see he felt terrible. He left me at the door and went home.

Several days later, he met me after class and again apologized and asked me to reconsider. He said drinking meant nothing to him, that he never would touch liquor again if only I would date him again.

After meditating about this, I decided to give him another chance. Insofar as I know, he never did take another drink again until some years after we were married. I truly believed him, and I believe he believed it himself.

However, I have seen that if one does not have the gospel in his heart and gospel standards for his own, other pressures exert themselves and can become more important. This is what happened to Fred as he began rising in the business world in the metropolitan area where we live—his business associates and colleagues included him in their cocktail parties, in their noon luncheons that included cocktails. He began by having one drink. He was honest enough to tell me about it. I felt very bad, reminded him of his promise, and suggested that he drink nonalcoholic drinks. He told me there were times when he did this, but somewhere along the way he decided it wasn't worth it.

There was a time when he drank with his business associates, but not when he was in my company. Then that phase ended, and he would sheepishly order a soft drink for me and an alcoholic drink for himself. Then it progressed to two for himself, and on upward. When I asked him to try to curtail the number for his own sake as well as mine and the children's, he answered by snapping his fingers in my face to summon the waiter, ordering what he pleased and as much as he pleased, and telling me to live my life and let him live his. "Living his own life" now included smoking, I learned.

My thoughts constantly returned to our courting days and early days of marriage and how completely I had believed in his well-meant promises—and how I had relied on his love and mine to mean so much, to be so complete, that living the Word of Wisdom would never be a problem. I was heartbreakingly wrong.

In order to be "compatible" with my husband socially, I attended numerous cocktail parties, nightclubs, and the types of entertainment that appealed to him. Occasionally he attended church parties with me, but these less and less as years went by. At first, I felt strong enough to be untouched by the environment in which I found myself, but a steady diet of it finally had a telling effect. It was wounding to my soul. It is difficult to associate often and become truly friendly with people whose standards are so foreign to one's own, when your husband's "best friend" tries to kiss you behind your husband's back when sober and openly when drunk, when everyone but you is becoming more and more intoxicated, and the pace grows faster and more frantic.

Invariably during those endless evenings I would mentally picture the righteous men in our ward and think of the priesthood and its power, how well they honored and valued it, and how, through observance of gospel principles and the priesthood training, ordinary men become superior; how none of that calibre would consider taking his beloved wife into places where drunkenness, profanity, and insults to her womanhood were the common rule. The contrast burned within me as I watched and evaluated, and I came to appreciate and love the gospel more than ever, to cling to it, and to see the so-called sophisticated night life for the sensuous, degrading thing these people made of it.

I decided I could not go on in this manner and explained calmly to my husband my reasons for desiring to find our entertainment more within Church activities or in places where the children could accompany us. I expected at least a degree of cooperation. His answer was that if I would not go with him, he would go without me. I tried it, and he did go, and I spent miserable evenings at home with the children, trying to present to them that all was well while my mind raced wildly to the environments where I pictured Fred without me. It is agony, I learned, not to have a basic trust and belief.

I consulted the bishop, and he advised me to continue to go with Fred, or a situation might arise where he would be tempted to take someone else in my stead. He gave me a blessing to provide me with additional strength to save my marriage and still be true to my ideals. It helped immeasurably. Shortly thereafter, my husband suffered a setback in his career that left us short of extra funds. Thus our entertainment was curtailed. I looked upon it as a blessing, rather than a hindrance, and rejoiced.

Probably every person who faces the decision of whether or not to marry a nonmember thinks, "My love and I are different. I look at him and see the potential, and I know with us it will be different."

I remember how my mother pointed out to me instances of people who had made the decision to marry out of their faith, and how in most cases, the results were disillusioning. Some were divorced; some were living out their lives together in quiet desperation. There were many more marriages of this nature than those in which the partner had been converted and had proved valiant through the years. Statistics prove this point.

As young people we are not qualified to judge the potential. Upon what basis, except the desires of our hearts and a few outward indications in the beloved whom we are bound to see with "rose-colored glasses," can we claim that our marriage will be successful? Without the testimony that only the Holy Ghost can give us of the worthiness of a prospective mate, our opinions could be nothing more than wishful thinking.

The tremendous odds one faces then are these: If there is no conversion or only a partial one, the couple will be pulled farther and farther apart, especially if the member adheres to the teachings of the gospel, for in doing so, growth of the spirit is bound to occur through study and practice and through the influence of the Holy Ghost. Especially is this true of a person who hungers and thirsts after righteousness and, through growing, comes to a lively hope of eternal life.

The spiritual contrast in the two marriage partners becomes frightening to both parties.

The nonmember does not bask in the protective shadow of the believer and doer. Instead, the influences he invites into his life mold him, and if these are unrighteous, he is pulled in the other direction, making the gap between the two practically irreconcilable.

Mark well my experience, for it is not unique. Right around me are several men and women in our ward whose marriages, because they married nonmembers, are patterned much like ours, varying only in detail and degree. How many are there throughout the Church, then?

We not only ache at the negative experiences we must bear, but also for the loss of the positive blessings a unified living of the gospel generates in the home.

Improvement Era, October 1964, pp. 832ff.

Index